Why Should We Care?

A call to service among the sick, the hungry, the poor, and the homeless

New Sinai Press

by Dale A. Johnson

Library of congress Cataloging-in-Publication Data
New Sinai Press
Why Should We Care?
Missions, poverty, hunger, homlessness, Christianity

ISBN 978-0-6151-5415-2

Manufactured in the United States of America

First edition
August 2007

barhanna2001@yahoo.com

Dedicated to:

the incarnational heroes who live among the poor, the hungry, the sick, and the homeless, especially Jana and Bob at Dominican Crossroads, and to all who care for the disabled children at Mustard Seed Community in Cangrejo, Dominican Republic

Table of Contents

MILLENNIUM DEVELOPMENT GOALS

1. Eradicate extreme poverty and hunger

Halve the proportion of people living in extreme poverty by 2015.

Halve the proportion of people who suffer from hunger by 2015.

2. Achieve universal primary education

Ensure that by 2015, children everywhere, boys and girls alike, will be able to complete a full course of primary schooling.

3. Promote gender equality and empower women

Eliminate gender disparity in primary and secondary education, preferably by 2005, and in all levels of education no later than 2015.

4. Reduce child mortality.

Reduce by two-thirds the under-5 mortality rate by 2015.

5. Improve maternal health

Reduce by three-quarters the maternal mortality ratio by 2015

6. Combat HIV/AIDS, malaria and other diseases

By 2015 halt and begin to reverse the spread of HIV/AIDS
By 2015 halt and begin to reverse the incidence of malaria and other major diseases.

7. Ensure environmental sustainability

Integrate the principles of sustainable development into country policies and programs and reverse the loss of environmental resources.
Halve by 2015 the proportion of people without sustainable access to safe drinking water and basic sanitation
By 2015 achieve a significant improvement in the lives of at least 100 million slum dwellers.

8. Create a global partnership for development with targets for aid, trade and debt relief

Develop further an open, rule-based, predictable non-discriminatory trading and financial system Address the special needs both of the least developed countries and of landlocked and small island developing countries.

Deal comprehensively with the debt problems of developing countries through national and international measures in order to make debt sustainable.

In cooperation with developing countries, develop and implement strategies for decent and productive work for youth.

In cooperation with pharmaceutical companies, provide access to affordable essential drugs in developing countries}

In cooperation with the private sector, make available the benefits of new technologies, especially information and communications.

These goals are not a fantasy, says economist Jeffrey Sachs. "Ours is the first generation in the history of the world with the ability to eradicate extreme poverty. We have the means, the resources and the know-how. All we lack is the will."

Millions around the world are trapped in a relentless, hopeless poverty that kills people -- that allows children and their parents to suffer and die from starvation, disease and political neglect.

Jesus would be appalled by poverty this extreme, and by Christians who are indifferent to it.

Introduction: Why Should Christians Care?

For the first time in the history of humanity on earth there are more people living in cities than in rural settings. What are the challenges to bringing God's reign to the slum community? What are the questions and challenges we face? Why should we care?

The Sick

You would care if you knew what is it like as a 10 year old to live on the streets of Puerto Plata, Dominican Republic, Kolkata, India or Freetown, Sierra Leone? Some estimate there are 100 million children who live their lives attempting to avoid abusive adults by living in communities of kids, surviving together in our world's cities. Most of them are sick with parasites from bad water. Or what about women who live in the midst of drugs, violence, prostitution while trying to care for each other. Most of them are diseased with HIV/AIDS and other STDs. If you knew what is it like to hear stories of life on the streets from the perspective of those who work day in and day out amongst our world's abandoned street children and desperate women then you would care.

We must care because this is our call as Christians. More than that, it is our call as authentic human beings. We must care because they are us.

The Hungry

We should care about the hungry because one out of every three children in the world is either malnourished or so hungry that their life is at risk, and until this is changed your soul can never be fed. Do you not think that the cravings of the first-world culture, often expressed in drug addiction, is somehow related to the real hunger of others?

The Poor

We should care about the poor because we can eliminate extreme poverty in the world in our lifetime? It is a moral crime that we do not lead the way if we claim to believe in a good God.

We should care because poverty is a subject of many classes and books but it means nothing until many of us make it a point to intertwine our lives with the poor. It means that we are not transformed until others are transformed.

The Homeless

We should care because one billion people are living in squatter communities on land they do not own.

We should care because until they have adequate homes we are homeless in our spirit.

Incarnational Lives

We should care because there are those who point the way and serve as models for us such as Father Ben Beltran a Catholic priest who has lived and served for more than 30 years among dumpsite scavengers in Manila, Philippines. In his years of service and worship among garbage dumps he has discovered truths about himself, about God, about the poor and about the need to steward our environment. Currently he is building the "greenest" church in the world in a garbage dump, complete with solar power and dry composting toilets. Learn about Father Ben's journey, his love for God's creation, and his life of service among some of the most desperately poor on earth and then you might care.

We should care because for the first fifteen centuries of the Christian faith, most missionaries were radical monks and nuns who had pledged to serve the church through a missionary order. The Franciscans, the Jesuits, the Nestorians of the east and the ancient Celtic orders were essentially missionary bands made up predominantly of people who had taken vows in order to bring the gospel to the least and the lost. We learn from these ancient "mission agencies. We can learn that the mission has never changed. It is our most basic obligation as a Christian and as a compassionate human being to serve the sick, the poor, the hungry, and the homeless.

As members of a movement without membership we discover ourselves to be part of a radical postmodern movement.

It is clearly a movement of spiritual transformation. It is a return to the ancient call in a new world. Sometimes it can appear to be lightweight, but there is substance and there is focus in what is sometimes also called the Emerging Movement.

Many of the evangelical churches in America have highjacked the faith. It is a toxic Christianity that has adopted the ways of the first-world culture of materialism, globalism, and entertainment. It has forgotten its obligation to the poor, the pilgrim, and the stranger. It has lost its mission to open the eyes of the blind, the ears of the deaf, and recovery to the lame. And I am not just talking about the physically blind, deaf, and lame I am talking about the people who live in darkness because the rich turned off the lights, who suffer in silence because the privileged have shut the door, and those who are too weak to walk because food has been put out of their reach.

This is a call to a radical kind of Christianity that is ancient and part of the future church. I know that I am not alone. There are many who have shown up at the foot of the mountain and are ready to climb.

To What are We Called to Do?

Serve the Sick

HIV/AIDS

The extent of human suffering brought about by the global HIV/AIDS pandemic has rarely been seen before in the history of the world. HIV/AIDS is increasingly a disease of the young and the most vulnerable, particularly girls. AIDS has orphaned 14 million children and left millions more extremely vulnerable. Statistics available from 2002 show that 720,000 babies became infected with the virus during the mother's pregnancy, during birth or through breastfeeding.

And yet, a single dose of a triple cocktail of HIV drugs can reduce the transmission of HIV to the unborn child by 80%. Where is the Christian community, especially the anti-abortionists, who claim that the life of an unborn child is so sacred? Shame on all of us, no matter what our views on abortion, for not acting sooner.

The scourge of AIDS is not unlike the group of diseases known to ancient peoples as leprosy. Like AIDS, leprosy was associated with poverty, stigma and uncleanness; it marked the sufferer as one to be marginalized, cast aside by the community. Fear of contagion and the social isolation of disease meant one's friends, neighbors and even family averted their eyes and kept their distance just when help and support were needed most.

14

In Jesus' time lepers lived separately from the community in a kind of quarantine but without any care or support from the community. They were cast out and shunned. The disease was contagious, so the community was protecting itself, but the cost borne by the sufferers was enormous. Not only were they ill and prohibited from earning a living, but they also were cut off from the normal social systems of support and identity that would have been available to others.

South African theologian Denise Ackerman asks, "What does it mean to confess to being the 'one holy, catholic, and apostolic church' in the midst of the 'bleak immensity' of the HIV/AIDS crisis?" She suggests:

> If we are truly one, we are the church with HIV/AIDS. People living with HIV/AIDS are found in every . . . religious denomination. We are all related; what affects one member of the Body of Christ affects us all. We are all living with HIV/AIDS. There is no "us" and no "them." We dare not forget that inclusion, not exclusion, is the way of grace. If we are holy, we are not living some superhuman mode of existence . . . Holiness is not withdrawal from the smell of crisis, sickness, or poverty, but engagement, often risky, in situations where God is present. If we are catholic, we are in solidarity because we are connected, in communion, with those who are suffering and who experience fear of rejection, poverty and death. If we are apostolic, we stand in continuity with the church in its infancy ... This means that we are zealous for the Word, and that we continuously examine the ideals of the early church and measure ourselves against them. This

is nothing new. It is simply a call to put the words of the creed into practice.

Inclusion, engagement, connectedness and continuity -- these are the values Ackerman calls the church to live out as it lives with AIDS.

How did Jesus respond to a sufferer of a deadline and stigmatizing disease? As we see in Luke 5:12-14. We see that Jesus included the leper, engaged him, connected with him and brought him back into the continuity of their shared tradition.

Jesus included the leper by accepting the leper's request to be in relationship. "If you choose," beseeched the leper; "Yes, I do choose," said Jesus. Jesus engaged the leper by stretching out his hand. He actively reached toward him, closing the physical distance by his action. Jesus connected to the leper by touching him, shocking the leper and Jesus' followers alike, and violating the norms of their shared culture. Jesus brought the leper back into continuity with their community by telling him to abide in their tradition's requirements and so return to life in community.

This story gives us an image of what it might mean to be the church with HIV/AIDS. If we follow Jesus' example we will be inclusive, engaged, connected and in continuity with those most ill and most vulnerable because of poverty.

Is there Hope for HIV/AIDS?

The HIV rates vary greatly in Africa, and so must the sexual patterns too! There are 20-fold higher HIV rates in Zambia compared to Senegal!

The male culture in highly affected areas of Southern Africa is that of many small houses, i.e simultaneous sexual relations with several young women. Many men in the Dominican Republic are used to having as many sex partners as their economy could allow. That must and will stop, because now people are now dying!

In the Dominican Republic and even Haiti. Hunger, disease, poverty can all be eradicated on this island. There are case studies all around us offering solutions.

Poverty, real poverty, is when you do not have enough to eat, clean water to drink, or money to pay the rent. Desperation sets in and you think about selling your child. Does it happen? Yes it does, especially when a mother is sick from HIV.

I have been compiling a report about the plight of children in the Dominican Republic where I work, collecting testimony from various sources and following up with confirmation. Some mothers have sold their children. They are just too sick to take care of them. I have interviewed eight women recently and checked on their stories and have been horrified so see that children have been sold to the sex trade, some have been used in insurance scams as bodies to put in cars that purposely get into accidents, and only a few have been sold to people who will actually care for them and give them a better life. We are asked all the time here if we know of children who can be adopted. Generally I am against it because it is subject to corruption and is another form of human trafficking, especially when the child is adopted out of country. Now I know there are wonderful people who could not imagine adopting a child themselves for any other reason than love and compassion. But the bad people seem to have more money and they can out bid the good people and often this happens. I generally favor internal adoptions where the child is adopted into a family in his own country. It happens a lot here. Dominicans are very family oriented and most of these adoptions are informal and loving. But CONANI, the national organization charged for the welfare of children and the judges and courts associated with them, should always be involved and we encourage this when we run into desperate people who want to sell their children. Unless they will do it through a judge or CONANI and a lawyer who is working for the interest of the child we will not get involved.

It is far better to find help to treat the mother and keep the family together. It is better to help the mother feel well enough to continue to care for her children. Recently one mother I know with HIV sold her child and she soon died. I do not think she died from HIV/AIDS so much as she died from a broken heart.

Disease, Corruption, Crime: it is all related!

Many children here in the Dominican Republic have homes. Yes they are nothing but scrap metal tin and a few broken boards. But the kids who are homeless do not even have this. Yesterday at the feeding center in

Puerto Plata; we did not have many kids show up. The police made a sweep of the area because the kids were bothering the tourists according to the police. So the kids sit a jail for a day. A few of the kids went to the new market and one boy was telling me that his mother needs medicine. If he does not sell boiled eggs the mother does not get her medicine. From what I could determine the mother has diabetes. I went to see her and I asked her if she has an identity card. It was a fake identity card probably sold to her by some human trafficker. She is an illegal alien from Haiti so she has no access to clinics here but she can go to the pharmacy. Marta has suggested we make identity cards for the kids showing that they belong to our organization and are beneficiaries. It is not a legal document but the police and school officials have respected it in the past when I have shown them pictures from our database and have turned the kids back to us."

HIV/AIDS: Modern Leprosy

"I don't have the money or the strength to go to the capital where I might get help," says Ladi who is HIV-positive and seriously ill. "When the fever, the headache hit me I get scared and I think I am going to die."

For fear of rejection, Ladi hasn't told her family that she is HIV-positive, and the doctor has nothing to offer her but vitamin pills which she cannot afford.

The countryside is green and fertile all the way to Ladi's *batey* – community of workers on the sugar cane plantations. But four hours' drive from the capital, Santo Domingo, the *batey* lacks clean water, work and often hope for the future.

Ladi's story illustrates the Dominican Republic's failure to fulfill its human rights obligation to ensure access to health care and treatment for people living with   HIV/AIDS.

The international community spends millions of dollars on supporting the prevention and treatment of HIV/AIDS in the Dominican Republic, yet the authorities often fail in their efforts to organize help. It does not reach the people who need it the most.

Leticia was working in the Free Zone of Esperanza when the company made all their workers take a blood test. She was not told what it was for. Before she understood what was going on, her boss and colleagues knew that she was HIV-positive. She lost her job.

"I didn't realize that they had forced me to take an HIV test. And it was a shock to learn that I was positive. Being fired was of course another shock," She says. But she chose to fight back. "I... tried to file a suit against the company. The company fired 80 people after this test."

We have received numerous reports of compulsory HIV tests at work and before getting a job; no confidentiality about the tests and the results; if the test is positive you are fired.

HIV-positive people from other towns reportedly had

similar experiences, suggesting that discrimination in the labor market is common.

In a resort town , wealthy tourists enjoy a relaxing holiday while just a few minutes away, Marime, aged 29 and a mother of eight, lies sick in the hospital. She has lived and worked in the resort area all her life. I visited her abandoned home: a shack with a leaking tin roof and a ragged mattress. She had been found half dead from starvation and illness. She was taken to hospital, dehydrated and unable to care for her three-year-old child who was left naked, sick and alone. The hospital confirmed that she was HIV-positive and sick, but gave her no treatment. Nobody took care of her child.

"At the public hospitals in this country there is widespread discrimination against people living with HIV. The doctors often refuse to treat us because they are scared," she says.

The local SIDA clinic confirms that many doctors refuse to treat HIV-positive patients. Without access to sterile gloves, running water and routines for dealing with accidents, they run a high risk of being infected when treating HIV-positive people. In the private medical sector this is not a problem.

HIV/AIDS workers often report receiving frequent death threats over the phone and have been followed by unregistered cars at night."

Disease

A recent medical team from the states found about 43% of the street children recently interviewed has significant medical conditions. Among these conditions was a surprising number of burn injuries. Much of this is directly attributable to poverty. The poor here cannot afford propane or electricity. Most people here cook with propane. But the poor make their own charcoal. This includes not only Haitian immigrants to the DR but also poor Dominicans. These open fires around children lead to a significant number of injuries. People use cans, metal buckets, and anything metal to burn wood slowly to reduce it to charcoal. This resulting residue is a long burning source of fuel for cooking. Children often end up as the victims of their own curiosity and proximity to these makeshift stoves. Of course when they get burned they do not have the money to go to a clinic and suffer and great deal of pain and scarring.

Water

I do not think there is anything more important than clean water in regard to human health. It is fundamentally the single most important thing that can be done for a people. I was talking to a couple of doctors the other day about this who were treating many of the poor of Puerto Plata. More than half the children and mothers suffer from a water related problem. Diarrhea, dysentery, stomach problems from contaminated food were just a few of the things that are directly associated with lack of clean water. What good does it do to give a child a mild pesticide to rid him of parasites in his gut when he we reintroduce them again by drinking bad water? Water born diseases lead to more severe problems such as dysentery, malaria, typhus, and other water born diseases that are highly contagious.

The first responsibility for clean water points to the government. But most solutions are capital intensive and the government often does not have the more for expensive filtration plants. NGOs have worked for years on the island drilling wells and introducing sand filtration systems. The trouble is that many of the aquifers are polluted. So no mater how deep you drill you still are on an island where pollution potential is great.

Private companies filtrate water and the poor are often not able to afford it. But this is the most immediate and quick solution. Yet programs like this must have long term and sustained solutions.

Serve the Hungry

The right to food is one of the principles enshrined in the 1948 Universal Declaration of Human Rights.

The 1969 Declaration on Social Progress and Development declared the need for "the elimination of hunger and malnutrition and the guarantee of the right to proper nutrition." Likewise, the Universal Declaration on the Eradication of Hunger and Malnutrition, adopted in 1974, declared that every person has the inalienable right to be free from hunger and malnutrition for their full development and to preserve their physical and mental capacities. In 1992 the World Declaration on Nutrition recognized that access to suitable, wholesome and safe food is a universal right.

These words leave no room for doubt. The public conscience has spoken out unambiguously. Yet millions of people are still marked by the ravages of hunger and malnutrition or the consequences of food insecurity. Is this due to a lack of food? Not at all! It is generally acknowledged that the resources of the planet, taken as a whole, are sufficient to feed everyone living on it. Indeed, the per capita availability of food worldwide has even increased by about 18 percent over the past few years.

The challenge facing the whole of humanity today is certainly economic and technological in character, but it is more specifically an ethical, spiritual and political challenge. The challenge is as much a matter of practical solidarity and authentic development as it is of material advancement.

The human being can only discover or pursue truth, goodness and justice using his own faculties if his awareness is enlightened by a deeper universal consciousness. It is precisely this consciousness that enables human nature to consider disinterested duty toward others. Christians believe that it is divine grace which gives human beings the strength needed to act according to their own discernment.

Solving the problem of hunger is an obligation not only for Christians but also for all people of good will to accomplish this gigantic task. 'Feed the man dying of hunger, because if you have not fed him, you have killed him.' Such a solemn warning urges everyone to be firmly committed to combating hunger.

God challenged Cain, asking him to account for the life of his brother Abel: "What have you done? The voice of your brother's blood is crying to me from the ground" (Gn. 4:10). This is our challenge today.

It is certainly not an unfair or aggressive exaggeration to apply these almost unbearable words to the plight of our contemporaries who today are starving to death. These words spell out a priority and are intended to touch our consciences.

The issue which needs to be faced depends on the economic and political policies of those who lead and manage, but also those of producers and consumers. The answers are deeply rooted in our own lifestyles.

Reality of Hunger

Our planet should be able to feed everyone adequately. Before taking up the challenge of hunger, the many facets and the real causes of hunger must be examined. However, there is no exact understanding of all the situations of hunger and malnutrition that exist in the world. Several major causes have nevertheless been identified.

Until the 19th century, famines which decimated whole populations were more often the work of nature. Today they may be not so vast, but in most cases are human-made. One need only cite a few regions or countries to be convinced: Ethiopia, Cambodia, the former Yugoslavia, Rwanda, Haiti, etc. At a time when humanity is better equipped than ever before to deal with hunger, such situations are a true disgrace to humanity.

The great efforts that are now being deployed have brought some benefits, but the fact remains that malnutrition is more widespread than hunger and takes widely different forms. A person can be malnourished without being hungry. Yet the organism's physical, intellectual and social potential is impaired just the same. Malnutrition may be due to food quality or a poorly balanced diet (by excess or lack of). Often it is also due to not having enough to eat and becomes acute when there is a shortage of available food. Some call this "denutrition" or "undernutrition". Malnutrition encourages the dissemination of some infectious and endemic diseases and aggravates their consequences. Further, it increases mortality rates, particularly among children under 5 years of age.

The fact of being poor almost invariably means falling more easily prey to the many hazards that threaten survival and being less resistant to physical sickness. Since the '80s, poverty has grown increasingly more serious and is threatening ever-larger numbers of people in most parts of the world. Within a poor population, the first victims are always the weakest individuals: children, pregnant women, nursing mothers, the sick and the elderly. There are also other vulnerable groups that run a very high risk of malnutrition: refugees and displaced persons as well as victims of political turmoil.

But it is in the 42 least-developed countries—of which 28 are in Africa alone—that hunger is most severe. "About 700 million people in developing countries—20 percent of their population—still do not have access to enough food to meet their basic daily needs for nutritional well-being.

In the developing countries, it is commonplace for populations whose livelihood depends on low-yielding subsistence agriculture to suffer from hunger during the interval between two harvests. When earlier harvests have also been insufficient, food shortages can occur and give rise to an acute phase of malnutrition. This weakens the population physically, placing them at risk just when all their energy is required to prepare for the next harvest. Food shortages place the future of these people in jeopardy since they eat crop seeds, plunder natural resources and accelerate soil erosion, degradation or desertification on their lands.

In addition to the distinction between hunger (or famine) and malnutrition, there is a third type of situation-—food insecurity—which leads to famine or malnutrition by making it impossible to plan and implement any long-term measures to foster and attain sustainable development.

Climatic factors and disasters of all kinds, however consequential, are far from being the sole causes of hunger and malnutrition. In order to deal effectively with the problem of hunger and all its causes, whether contingent or permanent, the linkages between them should be considered.

Economic Causes

The primary cause of hunger is poverty. Food security essentially depends upon an individual's purchasing power and not the physical availability of food. Hunger exists in every country. It has resurfaced in European countries, West and East alike, and is very widespread in countries that are insufficiently and incorrectly developed.

However, the history of the 20th century shows that economic poverty is not inevitability. Many countries have taken off economically and are continuing to do so at this very moment. At the same time still others are foundering after falling prey to national or international policies based on false premises.

Hunger stems simultaneously from:

a) Poorly managed economic policies in every country, since unsound policies implemented in the developed countries indirectly, but strongly, affect all the economically poor people in every country.

b) Structures and customs that are ineffective or which are blatantly destructive of national wealth:

—At the domestic level in developing countries—the large public or private organizations enjoying monopoly status (which is sometimes inevitable) often hamper development instead of fostering it as demonstrated by the adjustments undertaken in many countries over the past 10 years.

—At the domestic level in developed countries-shortcomings are less noticeable at the international level, but are no less damaging, directly or indirectly, to all the world's deprived.

—At the international level—constraints on trade and economic incentives are often ill conceived.

c) Morally reprehensible conduct such as the craving for money, power and a public image, as ends in themselves, is evidenced by a diminished sense of public service for the sole benefit of individuals or worthy groups; this is accompanied by a high level of corruption in a variety of different forms, from which no country may fairly claim to be exempt.

All this reveals the contingent nature of human activities. For despite the best intentions, mistakes are often committed, creating unstable situations. Pointing them out is one means of setting about to resolve them.

The root cause of non-development is the lack of will and ability to freely serve humanity, by and for each human being, which is a fruit of love. This is something that runs throughout this entire complex situation: at every level of technology in the broad sense of the term, in structures, legislation and in moral conduct. It is manifested in the design and performance of acts and instruments whose economic scope may be either broad or narrow.

The lack of skills, structures that are no longer capable of serving cost-effectively, individual moral deviance and the absence of love are the causes of hunger. Shortcomings in terms of any one of these points, anywhere in the world, inevitably lead to a further reduction in the share rightfully due to the hungry.

Recent economic and financial developments throughout the world are an illustration of these complex phenomena. Technology and morality are closely implicated in them and determine economic performance. This leads us to the question of the debt crisis in the majority of the third world countries along with the adjustment measures that have been or are about to be implemented.

The unilateral massive rise in oil has far-reaching repercussions on the non-oil-producing countries. The releasing of massive volumes of liquid funds that the banking system endeavored to recycle caused a general economic slowdown as a result of which the poor countries suffered considerably. For a variety of reasons, during the '70s and '80s most countries were able to borrow heavily at variable rates of interest, and the countries of Latin America and Africa were able to develop their public sector to an exceptional degree. This period of easy money led to many excesses: unnecessary projects, which were poorly designed or badly implemented, the wholesale destruction of traditional economies and the spread of corruption in every country. Some countries in Asia managed to avoid these mistakes and were able to develop very rapidly.

Soaring interest rates—caused by the mere interplay of unbridled and probably uncontrollable market forces—placed most of Latin America and Africa in a position of having to withhold debt repayments. This caused a flight of capital abroad, which in the short term posed a threat to the local social fabric, in many cases already mediocre and vulnerable, and also threatened the very existence of the banking system. That made it possible to gauge the extent of the damage caused in every sphere: economic, structural and moral. Purely technical and organizational solutions were initially sought. But such measures, which are necessary when sound, need to be supported by a thorough overhaul of behavior on the part of everyone, particularly people who, in every country and at all levels, are able to evade the enormous constraints which poverty imposes on decisions regarding their lives.

There is a conclusion to be drawn from this: Human advancement depends on the human being's capacity to practice altruism, love in other words, which has extremely important practical implications. In succinct and realistic terms, love is not a luxury. It is a condition for the survival of a very large number of human beings.

Socio-cultural Causes

Certain socio-cultural factors have been shown to increase the risks of famine and chronic malnutrition.

Food taboos, the social and family status of women—their real influence within the family, the lack of training for mothers in feeding and nutrition techniques, widespread illiteracy, and insecurity regarding work and unemployment—are some of the factors that can accumulate and cause malnutrition as well as dire poverty. Let us keep in mind that not even the developed countries themselves are immune to this scourge. The same factors create occasional or chronic malnutrition on the part of many of the "new poor" just as they are beginning to catch up with the others who live in affluence and over-consumption.

Ten thousand years ago the world probably had a population of 5 million. In the 17th century, with the dawning of the modern age, it had reached 500 million. Then the demographic growth rate began to rise more steeply: to 1 billion by the beginning of the 19th century, 1.65 billion at the beginning of the 20th, 3 billion in 1964, 4 billion in 1975, 5.2 billion in 1990, 5.5 billion in 1993, and 5.6 billion in 1994. For a time, the demographic situation developed differently between the "affluent" and the "developing" countries. This situation is still evolving. Let us not forget that proliferation is a reaction by nature-and consequently by the human being-to threats to the survival of the species.

Research has shown that as peoples and nations become more affluent high birth rates and high death rates are reversed to low birth rates and low death rates. The transition period may be critical in terms of food resources, because the death rate falls before the birth rate. Technological changes must accompany population growth; otherwise the regular agricultural production cycle regular agricultural production cycle is broken due to the depletion of the soils, the reduction of fallow periods and the lack of crop rotation.

Hunger and Population Growth

Is rapid population growth a cause or a consequence of underdevelopment? Except in extreme cases, population density cannot account for hunger. Let us look first at the following facts. It was in the overpopulated deltas and valleys of Asia that the "green revolution" agricultural innovations were first applied. Yet countries with small populations like Zaire or Zambia, which could have fed a population 20 times the size of their own without requiring any major irrigation schemes, are still short of food. The reason lies in the skewed measures imposed by governments and in economic management and policies, not in any objective causes or economic poverty. Today it is said that there is a greater chance of reducing excessive demographic growth by trying to reduce mass poverty than there is of combating poverty merely by reducing the population growth rate.

The demographic situation will only evolve slowly so long as families in the developing countries believe that their production capacity and their security can only be guaranteed by having a large number of children. It should once again be reiterated that it is generally economic and social changes that enable parents to accept the gift of a child. In this area, developments depend to a very large extent on the parents' socio-cultural background. Thought should therefore be given to educating couples in responsible planning of family size and the spacing of births in full respect for moral and ethical principles and in harmony with the true nature of the human being.

Political Causes

Depriving people of food has been used throughout history and is still used today as a political or military weapon. In some cases this is a veritable crime against humanity.

Yet there have been many such cases in the 20th century, such as:

a) Stalin's systematic withholding of food from Ukrainian peasants around 1930, causing the deaths of some 8 million people. This crime, which remained unknown, or almost, for a long time, was confirmed with the opening up of the Kremlin archives.

b) The sieges in Bosnia, particularly of Sarajevo, when even humanitarian aid itself was held hostage.

c) The resettlement of whole populations in Ethiopia to enable the one-party government to gain political control. Hundreds of thousands of people died as a result of the famine caused by forced migration and by abandoning the crops.

d) The cutting off of food to Biafra in the '70s was used as a weapon against political secession.

The collapse of the Soviet Union has helped to remove one of the causes of civil wars, the provocation by direct Soviet intervention or reaction to its intervention including: revolutions resolving nothing, displaced populations, the breakdown of organized agriculture, tribal strife and genocide. However, many situations still remain, or have reemerged, which could give rise to the same phenomena once again. Even though possibly not on the same scale, these are no less damaging to the people. Today's situations are mainly a matter of resurgent nationalism being fostered by a few ideologically driven regimes, local repercussions of struggles for influence between the developed countries and power struggles in certain countries, especially in Africa.

Also noteworthy are the embargoes imposed for political reasons against countries such as Cuba or Iran. These are regimes deemed to be a threat to international security, which keep their own people hostage. Indeed, it is the people themselves who are the first to fall victim to such acts of force. This is why the costs, in humanitarian terms, of such decisions must be carefully taken into account. Furthermore, some leaders play on the misery of their people, brought about by their actions, in order to force the international community to resume supplies. These are situations that have to be dealt with on a case-by-case basis in the spirit of the World Declaration on Nutrition, which states, "food aid must not be denied because of political affiliation, geographic location, gender, age, ethnic, tribal or religious identity."

Last, political actions can also have repercussions in terms of hunger. On a number of occasions we have seen developed countries with agricultural surpluses exporting these surpluses (for example wheat) free of cost to countries whose staple diet is rice. The purpose is to underpin domestic commodity prices. These free exports have had very negative effects, altering the people's eating habits and discouraging the local farmers, who need to be strongly encouraged to produce more.

Economic Malaise

Economic disparities within the developing countries are greater than those that exist in developed countries or even between the countries themselves. Wealth and power are highly concentrated in a restricted but complex section of society that is in contact with the international arena and is able to control the state apparatus, which is itself full of shortcomings. This holds up all chance of improvement and even causes economic and social decline.

Differences in living standards not only give rise to conflict, which can lead to a spiral of violence, but these differences further encourage patronage as the only means of achieving personal self-fulfillment. As a result, all purely economic initiatives are paralyzed, while the altruism that exists in all traditional societies is seriously jeopardized. In such situations, the state often has a major part to play, enabling it to encourage the export sector, which is good in itself— but leaving little profit for the local people as a whole.

Traditional food crops are often threatened by poorly targeted economic development. For example, traditional commodities are being replaced by industrial agriculture for both export (large volumes of agricultural commodities are earmarked for export and are dependent upon international agricultural markets) and local substitute commodities (for example, sugar cane in Brazil to produce alcohol for vehicle fuel in order to reduce oil imports has caused the migration of large numbers of uprooted peasants).

Earth Can Feed All Its Inhabitants

Between 1950 and 1980, total world food production doubled, and at the present time "globally there is enough food for all." The fact that people continue to starve despite this shows that the problem is structural and that "inequitable access is the main problem." Hunger is not a problem of availability, but of meeting demand. It is an issue of poverty.

Developing production capacities has much more to do with disseminating advances in production techniques (progress in genetics and implementation). We note that Indonesia's average rice output has risen from 4 tons to 15 tons per hectare in the space of one generation, far outstripping its already record population growth rate. In most countries where agriculture is making progress, yields are improving to such an extent that output is increasing, sometimes very steeply, despite the sharp decline in the number of farmers.

Agricultural intensification generally requires substantial capital investment. But most of the developing countries still practice subsistence farming, based mainly on human "capital," with limited technical resources and difficulties in finding adequate water supplies. Even though the "green revolution" has been fairly successful, it has not managed to solve the food production problems for a large number of developing countries.

It is certainly possible to predict progress to improve intensive farming and to limit damage to the environment. But as in the developed countries, other production systems should be used which will better conserve natural resources and ensure widespread ownership of productive land. Crop and livestock farmers' associations, joint management of water supplies and the creation of cooperatives should be encouraged to move in this direction.

Ethical Challenges

In order to make progress with solving the problem of hunger and malnutrition throughout the world, it is indispensable to grasp the ethical nature of the whole issue.

If the cause of hunger is a moral evil, above and beyond all the physical, structural and cultural causes, the challenges are also of a moral nature. This is capable of motivating all men and women of good will who believe in the universal values of every culture, particularly

This challenge involves acquiring a better understanding of the phenomena, people's capacity for mutual service—which may be done merely through the interplay of well-understood economic forces and also doing away with corruption of every kind. Apart from all this, the challenge lies above all at the level of freedom for every person to cooperate in the advancement of all human beings and the integral human being in their daily work, namely, by working together to foster the development of the common good. This kind of development involves social justice and the universal destination of the goods of the earth, the practice of solidarity, peace and respect for the physical environment. This is the direction that must be taken in order to restore hope and build up a world that is more welcoming to future generations.

The huge task facing Christians everywhere is to foster conduct of this kind. Like a small amount of yeast in very hard dough, they are called by a close adhesion to the love, which our Lord has for all people: a love experienced in the very depths of one's being.

This exciting task is to set an example at every level: technical, organizational, moral and spiritual. It involves mutual assistance at every level of responsibility, which includes all those who are not "excluded" by their own social conditions.

Striving in this way for the common good must necessarily be underpinned by concern for and love of humanity. In the most varied situations, people are faced daily with the alternative between personal and collective self-destruction or love for our neighbor. Love for our neighbor therefore demonstrates our awareness that there is a responsibility from which one cannot shrink when faced with our own limitations or with the enormous magnitude of the duties to be performed out of love for all men and women. How would history judge a generation, which had all the means to feed the population of the planet and yet with fratricidal indifference refused to do so? Would a world in which poverty fails to encounter life-giving love not be a desert?"

Love is far more than mere giving. Development is cultivated through the work of those who have the greatest courage, the greatest competence and honesty. These leaders feel solidarity with all humanity, and humanity is affected, to a greater or lesser degree, whether near or far, by what these individuals do or should be doing. This concrete universal responsibility is an essential manifestation of altruism.

Solidarity is obviously a demand that is placed on all. Fortunately, it is not necessary to wait for the majority of humanity to be converted to love of their neighbor in order to gather the fruits of the work of those acting in their own particular situation without waiting. Hope must be drawn from the results of the work of such persons who, in their daily work at all levels, act in the service of the integral human being and of all humanity.

Pursuing these riches as an absolute good in themselves robs them wholly or partially of utility for the common good. The world economic system is globally mediocre (in comparison with the peak performances achieved in some countries for quite considerable periods of time), so costly in human terms (when it functions properly and where it does not function at all), paying dearly for bad habits and imposing a veritable moral yoke on people.

Conversely, as soon as groups of men and women begin working together in order to take due account of the need to serve the whole community and each individual member of it, remarkable developments can be achieved. People previously deemed rather useless become outstanding for the quality of their services, and a positive effect gradually improves the material, psychological and moral conditions of their lives. This is really the "obverse" of the "structures of sin." One might call them the "structures of the common good" which pave the way to the "civilization of man." Our experience in such situations gives some idea of what the world might be like if people were more concerned about the common interests and the fate of each man and woman in all they do and in the exercise of all their responsibilities.

Listen to the Poor in Order to Solve Hunger

If the poor, in the economic sense of the term, bear witness to the lack of concern for the common good, they have something specific to tell us.

They have their own opinions and experiences with regard to real daily life about which the better off know nothing. As John Paul II said in his encyclical letter *Centesimus Annus*:

"It will be necessary above all to abandon a mentality in which the poor—as individuals and as peoples—are considered a burden, as irksome intruders trying to consume what others have produced.... The advancement of the poor constitutes a great opportunity for the moral, cultural and even economic growth of all humanity."

The views of those living in poverty—which are no more accurate or complete than those of the leaders— are, however, essential to leaders if they desire to ensure long-term work which does not lead to self-destruction. Embarking upon difficult and costly social and economic policies without taking account of the perception of reality by the most humble members of society can eventually lead to extremely costly dead-ends for the whole world.

This is what has happened in the case of Third World debt. If the lenders and the borrowers had heeded the personal opinions of the poorest people, as one of the essential elements of reality, greater wisdom would have meant greater caution, and in very many countries the adventure would not have turned out so badly or it may have turned out well.

Considering the complexity of the problems to be solved, or rather the complexity of living conditions to be improved, giving preference to heeding the poor will prevent us from falling into the slavery of short-term perspective, technocracy, bureaucracy, ideology or idolatry regarding the role of the state or the role of the market. Each of these has its essential usefulness, but only as a means and never as an absolute end.

Intermediate entities have the main function of ensuring that the voices of those living in poverty are heard and of collecting their views, needs and desires. But these entities are often quite inadequate for the task, suffering either from the fact of occupying a monopolistic position which leads them to cultivate their own power or competing with others who seek to use the poor as a means of acquiring power. The work of the trade unions is therefore particularly necessary, verging on heroism when they strive to perform such an essential function without being destroyed or taken over.

Under these conditions, sharing becomes genuine cooperation and collaboration in which every person contributes to all that the human community needs. The poorest play their role, which is essential, particularly in view of the fact that in reality they are excluded. This is a paradoxical situation, which should not surprise the Christian.

The duty to give every person the same right of access to the indispensable minimum to live on does not stem merely from a moral imperative to share with the poor, which is already a major obligation. The duty is also to reincorporate those living in poverty into the community as a whole, which without them tends to whither and can eventually be destroyed. People living in poverty do not belong on the sidelines in a marginalized position. Everything must be done to prevent this. They must be placed at the very center of our concerns, at the center of the human family. It is there that the poor can play a unique role within the community.

The concept of justice rooted in human solidarity, and by that very characteristic requiring the strongest to come to the aid of the weakest, should guide our steps wherever the voice of the poor is heard, working to create a world in which justice, peace and charity are jointly guaranteed.

Societies cannot be properly built up by excluding some of their members. To be consistent, this evidently means that people living in poverty are also entitled to organize themselves so as to better obtain assistance for enabling them to free themselves from poverty.

Hunger and Violence

Lasting peace is not the result of a balance of forces, but of a balance of rights. Peace is not the fruit of the victory of the strongest over the weakest, but fruit of the victory of justice over unjust privileges, of freedom over tyranny, of truth over falsehood within and among peoples, of development over hunger, poverty or humiliation. In order to establish true peace and real international security, it is not sufficient to prevent war and conflict. Development must also be fostered, creating the right conditions to fully guarantee fundamental human rights. In this context, democracy and disarmament become two of the requirements of peace, which is indispensable for all genuine development.

Regional conflicts have cost the lives of about 17 million people in less than 50 years. "In the 1980s, world military expenditures grew to an unprecedented peacetime level; at an estimated [annual] $1 trillion [1 million], they accounted for roughly 5 percent of total world income."

This demonstrates the importance and urgent need for all political and economic leaders to ensure that the vast amounts of money earmarked for death, in the Northern Hemisphere as in the Southern Hemisphere, should henceforth be earmarked for life. Such an attitude would be the practical implementation of the moral grounds militating in favor of progressive disarmament. Such a course would also provide the opportunity to release substantial financial resources for the benefit of developing countries and vital for their authentic progress.

At present, nature is teaching all a lesson in solidarity that could easily be forgotten. In the very act of producing food, everyone discovers that they are either active or passive component parts of an ecosystem. A new sphere of responsibility is opening up to people's consciences.

Solutions

Develop a Culture of Giving

Human development will not come about as a result of economic mechanisms operating alone; a belief that all that is necessary is to encourage them. The economy will only become more human and humane if a whole range of reforms are carried out at every level. Designed to provide the best possible service for the genuine common good, these reforms must take an ethical approach based on the infinite value of each man and woman and of all humanity. That is an economy which allows itself to be inspired by "the need to build relationships between peoples on the basis of a constant 'exchange of gifts,' a real 'culture of giving' which should make every country prepared to meet the needs of the less fortunate."

Hunger and Food Aid

Emergency food aid deserves comment, since it is sometimes criticized for not tackling the root causes of hunger. Some view it as a humanitarian activity. Still others perceive it as a development lever, while some even consider it as a trade weapon. It is faulted for: discouraging local farmers; changing feeding habits;

being a tool for bringing political pressure to bear by creating dependency; arriving too late; fostering a free handout mentality; profiting ultimately only the middlemen; encouraging corruption and not getting through to the poorest people.

I n some countries food aid is extended endlessly, not without reason, and eventually becomes established as a structural fact. It then becomes a form of permanent balance of payments aid by reducing the national deficit. This aid can also be provided at a difficult period of structural adjustment as an accompanying measure, after consumption subsidies for basic commodities have been abolished. Emergency food aid must remain a temporary solution, and its purpose is strictly that of enabling people to survive through a crisis. As a humanitarian measure, it cannot in principle be challenged. It is only deviations in food aid that give rise to criticism.

Among these criticisms: It often arrives late or does not meet the real needs; its distribution is poorly organized or misdirected by political or ethnic factors or patronage; because of theft and corruption, the food does not always reach the poorest people. Other criticisms note that emergency food aid is sustainable structural aid that some consider to be a development lever, while others view it as a trade weapon, a factor which destabilizes production and feeding habits, causing dependency.

In reality, its effects can be both beneficial and harmful. Apart from the fact that it enables whole populations to survive, all its positive aspects—such as the infrastructure work that it makes possible, tripartite transactions and the buildup of reserves in the developing countries-should not be forgotten. Even if it is a weapon that can be used for good or ill, it cannot be ignored.

Despite the criticisms leveled against it, emergency food aid could be improved by concerted action between all the partners in the chain: governments, local authorities, non-governmental organizations and church associations. Aid could be limited in time and be much better targeted for the people who are really suffering from food shortages. Local products should be used whenever possible.

Above all, emergency aid must help to free populations from their dependency. In order to do this, in addition to having adequate infrastructure and local distribution capacities, aid must always be accompanied by projects to enable the affected populations to take precautionary measures enabling them to guard against future food shortages. In this way, emergency or relief aid, under certain conditions, may be considered as an outstanding act of international solidarity. For "this kind of assistance does not bring a satisfactory solution as long as conditions of extreme poverty are allowed to continue and become even more acute, conditions which lead to increased deaths due to malnutrition and hunger."

Hunger and Land Reform

Local food production is often hampered by poor land distribution and irrational land use. Over half the population in developing countries is landless, and this proportion is continually growing. Even though virtually all the developing countries have agrarian reform policies, few of them have actually implemented them. Moreover, the agricultural lands used by the multinational food corporations are almost solely used to feed the populations of the North. The exploitation of these lands is causing their depletion and exhaustion. It is urgently necessary to embark upon a "bold reform of the structures and new models of relations between governments and peoples."

Hunger and Education

Any dichotomy between education and development must be removed. These are such interdependent objectives and are so strictly linked to one another that both of them must be pursued together if sustainable results are to be forthcoming. It is a duty in solidarity to enable everyone to benefit from "an education ... suitable to the particular destiny of all."

Non-Government Organizations (NGOs)

Over the past few decades a number of organizations founded by volunteers have come into being, joining others already in existence, to serve individuals and populations in difficulty. These international organizations are often known as non-governmental organizations NGOs. They are held in high repute thanks to their dynamism.

These organizations have shown their courage in promoting the integral development of people living in poverty and in responding to emergency situations (famine and drought in this particular instance). They have experience in drawing attention to desperate situations, marshalling private and public resources and organizing relief in the field. Most of them have supplemented their battle against hunger over the years by embarking on a more forward-looking, longer-term activity to foster development. Their most evident successes include projects for new initiatives implemented locally and autonomously, and projects designed to strengthen local communities and institutions.

The international organizations have a twofold mission: awareness building and action. While the second of these is obvious, the first is often unknown. Yet the two are inseparable. Prime importance must be given to sensitizing people to the reality and causes of mal-development wherever they are. Attracting private resources and making more people aware of the issues are crucial. It is necessary to build up this grass-roots base in order to increase official development assistance and change the "structures of sin."

The international organizations must work as real partners with the groups they assist. This produces a form of solidarity with a brotherly and sisterly face in dialogue and mutual trust while respectfully listening to one another.

Use of Reason with Love

Lastly, and taking a broader perspective, it is necessary to collect information and surveys based on experience and observation in specific situations in order to build up a data bank containing practical descriptions of real life situations, of "structures of sin" and of "structures of the common good" from every point of view.

Last year we did a modern social census of children in Puerto Plata, Dominican Republic. No one in government had an idea of how many children were homeless and living on the street. There is a culture of denial in the Dominican Republic. The government is so anxious to get tourist dollars they will look the other way when it comes to environmental damage, sex abuse, human trafficking, and the plight of homeless children. Government officials have told us that these are not problems here. And yet when presented with evidence in the form of interview on camera and in the field, certified statements, they will admit to the problems but have no idea of the scope.

We thought we would find maybe 200 children in the resort city of Puerto Plata. We found over 600. We took pictures, asked basic questions about vital issues. Then we followed up the data to discover how accurate the responses we were given. Truth often suffers when poverty invades the heart. Many of the children said they had parents but in fact were sold to men who used them for slave labor on the beaches shining shoes and selling candy and eggs. It turned out that over two thirds of the children we being used in forced labor situations and not living with parents or going to school.

We turned this data over to government agencies that used it to identity children of greatest need. We also sent the data to other NGOs who used it in their programs of service to these homeless children. Jesus, after all taught us to be as wise as serpents and gentle as doves. in other words, to use reason with love.

Hunger and the Environment

The pretense of pretending to want to provide more food to more people and at the same time weaken agriculture cannot continue. Agriculture seems to be contributing more pollution (with the wholesale use of fertilizer, pesticides and machines) as it reaches the industrial stage, before having developed the capacity to work without polluting. In addition to the other elements necessary in life, the atmosphere, water, soil and the woodlands are all threatened by pollution, over-consumption, man-made de certification and deforestation. In the space of 50 years, half the tropical forests have been cleared, more often than not in the quest for more land or because of short-term policies to intensify farming in order to offset the debt burden. In the poorest regions, desertification is being caused by survival practices that actually are increasing poverty. These include overgrazing as well as felling trees and shrubs for cooking and heating.

It is urgently necessary to manage this planet in an ecologically sustainable manner. From the viewpoint of agri-food production, which is already substantial, there are two elements to be considered.

There is little appreciation of how dynamic the poor really are. To remedy this, a great many attitudes and practices—economic, social, cultural and political—have to be changed. When people living in poverty are excluded from taking part in drafting projects of relevance to them, history has demonstrated that, overall, little benefit is derived from such projects.

The solidarity of the human community must be built up. It will not be possible to learn to share our daily bread unless it is agreed to redirect our consciences and work throughout the whole of society. Such attitudes lead to genuine democracy.

Democracy is generally acknowledged to be essential to human development because it enables everyone to play a responsible part in the governance of society. Moreover, the two go together and the weakness of one can jeopardize the other. If the principle of equality yields to force, the place of the poor in society may be reduced to the bare minimum. A democracy is judged in terms of the way it manages to dovetail freedom and solidarity, radically distancing itself from absolute liberalism or other doctrines that deny the sense of freedom or which act as stumbling blocks to genuine solidarity.

Faced with misery and poverty, more people and groups are increasingly choosing to take part in community action everywhere. These initiatives must be strongly encouraged. At the present time, more countries are increasingly supporting people's participation. But in some places attempts are still being made to thwart these initiatives where they are a source of irritation—sometimes with very dire consequences—even though they are the indispensable foundations of genuine development.

The non-governmental organizations set up locally to undertake development work have encouraged the constitution of a new people-based civil society in many developing countries. These non-governmental organizations have devised a wide range of different ways to work together and provide support. Thanks to the impetus given by the people who have paved the way, many of the very poorest people are now able to break free of poverty and improve their plight in terms of hunger and malnutrition.

Over the last few years, international associations and new ecclesial communities have embarked on initiatives in the socioeconomic field. In combating hunger and poverty, those groups have been basing their work on the medieval guilds, and above all, the cooperative unions in the 19th century when advocates of the common good created institutions according to the spirit of the Gospel or based on social solidarity.

The first person to emphasize the need to create organizations for social advancement was the Quaker P.C. Plockboy (d. 1695). Other pioneers of notoriety are Felicite Robert de Lamennais (1782-1854), Adolf Kolping (d. 1856), Robert Owen (1771-1858) and Baron Wilhelm Emmanuel von Ketteler (1811-1877). Today associations are coming into being to advance the common good of society and to stave off selfishness, pride and greed, which are often the laws that govern community life. These experiences throughout history and the achievements of these new initiatives bode well for the future.

"One of the great successes of the non-governmental organizations has been to give the poor access to credit." This access by people living in poverty has become a defining practice today, thus enabling an informal subsistence economy to make progress toward the formation of a real grass roots economic fabric. Perhaps it is not yet possible to be able to calculate the gross national product accurately, but its importance also lies in that which it signifies and heralds. Supporting community initiatives and relying on local partners prevents the persistence of an aid-driven approach, making it possible to gradually lay the foundations for integral development.

Hunger and Women

Women play a primary role in combating hunger and fostering development, but their role is not always adequately acknowledged and appreciated. It is important to emphasize the essential role that women play in the survival of whole populations, especially in Africa.

Often it is the women who produce the bulk of food for their family. Particularly in the developing countries, they are responsible for providing their family members with a wholesome and balanced diet. However, women become the first victims of decisions taken without their knowledge, such as decisions to abandon particular food crops and local markets of which they are the main operators. Such treatment shows a failure to respect women and hampers development. Under these conditions, the transition to the market economy and the introduction of technologies can, despite the best intentions, make the drudgery of women even worse.

Malnutrition particularly affects women, who are the first to suffer. This has further repercussions on their childbearing and affects the health and education prospects of their young children.

But the purpose of this effort, to highlight the role of women in the fight against hunger and malnutrition and in favor of development, must form part of a more ambitious framework. It should be one designed to enhance the social status of women in the poor countries by providing them with greater access to health care, vocational training and credit. This will enable women to make their full contribution in increasing production, fostering development, and in the economic and political evolution of their countries.

Progress must, however, ensure that the roles of men and women are preserved without driving a wedge between them and without feminizing men or masculinizing women. As the status of women improves, as is hoped, sight should not be lost of the attention women must provide to newly created and developing life. Some developing countries are setting a positive example by curbing excesses that now occur in the West with regard to altering the sensitivity of women, without shutting women up in their traditional role. In this sphere, the mistakes made in the past must not be repeated by playing down traditional structures to boost Western models, which are particularly unsuitable for local situations if adopted without adjustment.

The richest countries have a major responsibility in the process of reforming the world economy. In recent times, at least, they have given priority to relations with countries undergoing economic takeoff—that is to say, the true developing countries—and also with countries in Eastern Europe whose development can pose a geographically close threat.

The rich countries have their own economically poor and need to embark on difficult reforms in their own territories. They are, therefore, tempted to relegate the economically poor in the developing countries to a secondary plane. "We are not responsible for the world's poverty," is something that one hears frequently in the globally rich countries.

If such an attitude were to become common, it would be both unworthy and shortsighted. All people, regardless of location, but particularly those who possess economic resources and wield political authority, must constantly allow themselves to be challenged by the poverty of the most deprived so that the interests of those living in poverty are taken into account in decision-making and action. This is an appeal addressed to everyone responsible for decisions affecting the developing countries.

It is also addressed to all in every country and at the international level who are de facto holding up the possibility of pursuing the common good in order to protect interests, which in themselves may be wholly legitimate. Protecting these vested interests in such countries may cause hunger to persist in some parts of the world without being able to accurately identify a causal link or even victims. That makes it easy to deny their existence. Other forms of conservatism, at other levels and in other places, can also contribute to these same bottlenecks.

The leaders of developing countries should not rely on some hypothetical international reform before embarking on reforms in their own countries. Such reforms are often needed, evidently, to foster some degree of economic takeoff. This takeoff does not depend on any specific recipes, but its requirements demand a bold and unflagging implementation of simple rules. Rules, which make it possible for those who are able to take sound initiatives to do so and to retain part of the rewards of the efforts. Further, they prevent persons incapable of drawing on national resources from being rewarded without regard for their own contribution.

Hunger: A Call To Love

The experience of daily life in every country of the world calls us, if we do not close our eyes, to look the hungry in the eye. In this look is the blood of our brothers and sisters crying out (cf. Gn. 4:10). We know that it is God calling out to us through the hungry.

In the groaning of the hungry, it is God who is hungry and who is calling. Being a disciple of God, who is self-revealing, the Christian is urged to heed the cries of the poor. It is a call to love.

According to the writers of the psalms, those songs of the Old Testament, "the poor" are identified with "the just," "the righteous," those who "seek God," "fear God," "trust in God," those who "are blessed," "his servants" and who "know his name."

The whole of the light of the poor under the first covenant converges toward the woman who forms the hinge between the two testaments, as if reflected in a concave mirror. In Mary, all the devotion to Yahweh and all the experience which guided the people of Israel shone forth and took flesh in the person of Jesus Christ. Her Magnificat is the hymn of praise which bears witness to Christ: the hymn of the poor whose wealth is God alone (cf. Lk. 1:46ff).

This hymn opens with an explosion of joy, expressing immense gratitude: "My soul magnifies the Lord and my spirit rejoices in God my Savior." But it is not for riches or power that Mary rejoiced. She saw herself as small, lowly and humble. This basic idea runs throughout her hymn of praise in total contrast to anything dealing with pride, or the thirst for power and wealth. Those who desire these things are "scattered," "put down from their thrones" and "sent empty away."

Jesus himself took up this teaching of his mother in his Gospel discourse on the Beatitudes. They open—and it is no coincidence—with the words, "Blessed are the poor." His words show what this new person is in opposition to the "wealth" which he criticizes.

It is to the poor that Jesus addresses his good news (cf. Lk. 4:18). The "allurement of wealth," conversely, prevents people from following Christ (cf. Mk. 4:19). We cannot serve two masters, God and mammon (cf. Mt. 6:24). Concern for the morrow is the sign of a pagan mentality (cf. Mt. 6:32). For Jesus, these are not just fine words. Indeed, he bore witness to them in his own life: "The Son of Man has nowhere to lay his head" (Mt. 8:20).

The biblical precept must not be distorted or disguised. It runs counter to the spirit of the world and to our natural sensitivity. Our nature and our culture are repelled by poverty.

People living in poverty and wealth alike sometimes refer to the poverty of the Gospel in cynical terms. Christians are then accused of wishing to perpetuate poverty.

There also exists a form of poverty caused by the conviction that the pursuit of technical and economic progress is enough to make each person more worthy to be called a human being. But soulless development cannot suffice for the human being, and an excess of wealth and affluence is as harmful to the person as an excess of poverty. It is in the "development model" created by the Northern Hemisphere and spreading throughout the Southern Hemisphere that the sense of religion and human values stand the risk of being overwhelmed by a mentality of consumption, sought after for its own sake.

God does not want people—namely, all men and women—to be poor, since our Creator cries out to all through each one of the poor. God tells us quite simply that the poor, like the rich who are blinded by their wealth, are mutilated beings. The poor are mutilated by circumstances which lie far from their control, while the rich are mutilated by their handfuls and with their collusion. Both are thereby prevented from finding that interior freedom to which God unceasingly calls all humanity.

By being "filled with good things," the poor are not given some selfish revenge against their ill fate, but are placed in a situation that ensures that their most fundamental capacities are not diminished. The rich who are "sent empty away" are not being punished for being rich, but they are relieved of the burden and the blindness caused by being too exclusively attached to goods of all kinds.

In this twofold healing process, the poor are called to heal their hearts wounded by injustice, which can lead them to hate themselves and others. The rich are called to stop feeling guilty and use that as an excuse not to act. They cover their ears, close their eyes and stifle their hearts, submerged under their worthless riches of money, power, image and pleasures of every kind. This gives them a narrow view of themselves and of others, and as they increase their possessions, their appetites continue to grow.

World hunger makes us identify the weaknesses of the human being at every level. The rationale of sin shows how sin—that evil lurking in the heart of every person—lies at the root of the miseries in society as a result of what might be called the "structures of sin." For the church, this is culpable egoism, the pursuit of wealth, power and glory regardless of the cost, challenging the very value of progress as such.

"For when the order of values is jumbled and bad is mixed with the good, individuals and groups pay heed solely to their own interests, and not to those of others. Thus it happens that the world ceases to be a place of true brotherhood and sisterhood. In our own day, the magnified power of humanity threatens to destroy the race itself."

Conversely, the love, which comes to dwell in the human heart, enables men and women to overcome their limitations and to act in the world by creating "structures of the common good." This encourages people around them to move toward a "civilization of love" and to attract others.

Thus the human being is called to reform his or her actions. This issue is of vital importance to the world. The person is led to this reformation of the heart by a movement of self toward the unification of the self and of the human community in love. This reform of the human being, the whole person, is radical in its depth and in what it entails, for the very essence of love is radical. Love does not suffer from division; it encompasses all the prompting of the person—acts and prayers, material goods and spiritual riches.

The conversion of the heart of everyone, of each and every human being, is God's proposal, which can profoundly change the face of the earth, wiping away the hideous marks of hunger, which disfigure part of its face. "Repent and believe in the Gospel" (Mk. 1:15) is the imperative which accompanies the proclamation of the kingdom of God and which brings about its coming.

Here is the promise, which Our Lord makes us: "You shall be clean from all your uncleanness and from all your idols I will cleanse you. A new heart I will give you, and a new spirit I will put within you; and I will take out of your flesh the heart of stone and give you a heart of flesh. And I will put my spirit within you, and cause you to walk in my statutes and be careful to observe my ordinances" (Ez. 36:25-27).

Let us not be misled by this magnificent biblical language. It is not an appeal to fine sentiments to bring about a mere material sharing, however worthwhile and effective that might be. It is the most far-reaching proposal that could ever be put to us. It is the proposal of God, who comes to offer each one of us liberation from our idols and to teach us to love. This commits our whole being, reunified in this way. Then we can overcome our fears and our selfishness in order to be attentive to our brothers and sisters and to serve them.

Our idols are all near us. They are our longings as individuals and as communities, whether we are rich or poor, for material goods, power, reputation and pleasure, viewed as ends in themselves. By serving these idols, the human being is enslaved and the planet impoverished (cf. No. 25). The profound injustice suffered by those who cannot meet the bare necessities of life is precisely the fact that they are forced by necessity to seek material goods above all else.

The heart of the poor Lazarus was freer than the heart of the evil rich man, and through the voice of Abraham God not only asks the unrighteous rich man to share his feast with Lazarus, but demands a change of heart and acceptance of the law of love in order that he become a brother to Lazarus (cf. Lk. 16:19ff).

It is by freeing us from our idols that God will enable us to set about transforming the world, not only by increasing riches of all kinds, but above all by directing the work of humanity toward the service of all. The world can then rediscover its original beauty, which is not only the beauty of nature on the day of creation, but also the beauty of the garden that was perfectly tended, tilled and rendered fertile by the human being at the service of one's brothers and sisters, in the loving presence of God and out of love for God.

"Fight hunger by changing your lifestyle" is the motto, which shows the people in the affluent country how to become the brothers and sisters of those living in poverty.

Wherever in the world God has placed them, Christians must respond to the call of those who are hungry by personally questioning their own lives. The call of the hungry urges one to question the meaning and the value of daily actions, to seek out the immediate and sometimes more remote consequences of professional and voluntary work, handicrafts and domestic work. Further, one must gauge the magnitude, which is much more concrete and wide ranging than could be imagined, of the consequences of all one does, even the most ordinary things, and hence appraise real responsibility.

St. Paul states unequivocally that "Jesus Christ ... though rich ... for your sake he became poor" (2 Cor. 8:16). Christ wished to make us rich through his poverty and through the love we must always show to those living in poverty.

Listening to God in the presence of the poor will open up the human heart and lead it to seek an ever-new personal encounter with God. This encounter, which God is seeking in a ceaseless search for all humanity and the whole human being, will continue along the daily path which gradually transforms the lives of those who agree to "open the door" to God, who humbly knocks (cf. Rv. 3:20).

Listening to God demands time with and for God. It is personal prayer. This alone enables the human being to have a change of heart and hence of deeds. The time taken up by God is not taken away from the poor. A strong and balanced spiritual life has never removed anyone from the service of their brothers and sisters. If St. Vincent de Paul (d. 1660)—who was so well known for his commitment to the poorest of the poor—was able to say, "Leave off your prayer if your brother asks you for a cup of tea," let us not forget that he prayed for seven hours a day, and it was on this that he built up everything he did.

Those who listen to their brothers and sisters and open up to God's presence and action will begin, little by little, to question their own habits of life. The race for affluence—which more and more people are joining in, often in a world of increasing poverty—will gradually give way to a greater simplicity of life, which is already a distant memory in so many countries. This becomes possible once again, and even desirable, as soon as concern for appearances is no longer a consumer's choice.

Last, those who thus agree to change their views in order to adopt the view that God has shown us in the words of Christ and to reflect on the consequences of our actions, whether apparently important or insignificant, will be enabled to place themselves at the service of the common good and of the integral advancement of all humanity and each and every human being.

Gradually freed of fears and purely material ambitions and enlightened as to the possible consequences of their own actions, wherever they may be, those welcoming the presence of God in every aspect of life will become artisans of the civilization of love. Working discreetly and in depth, their work will take on the character of a mission in which their talents must be exercised and developed. A mission where they are called to contribute toward reforming structures and institutions. This exemplary behavior will then encourage their neighbors to do likewise and to be essentially devoted to serving the dignity of all men and women and their common good.

"Take courage, all you people of the land, says the Lord; work, for I am with you" (Hg. 2:4-5). The Christian then becomes a combatant against the "structures of sin" and even their agent of destruction. This will ensure that anything that hampers social and economic development will be less widespread. In regions where Christians lead men and women of good will with courage and determination, poverty can be halted in its tracks, consumption habits can be changed, reforms implemented, solidarity can flourish and hunger recede.

Christians are at the service of their brothers and sisters in every aspect of their work and their lives. Love put into practice appeals to all Christians in their daily work and in their personal initiatives. The commitment of Christians, like their humanitarian and charitable work, stems from the same call to mission.

In their paid work and in their unpaid voluntary work or working at home, which is often heavy, men and women are called to live the same mission, to manifest the good news and serve it through their daily sufferings and joys and in every situation. The quality of their work, participation in just reforms, humble behavior, concern for others, which is always present regardless of personal and lawful institutional objectives—all this is the daily lot of men and women seeking an opportunity in every aspect of their lives to allow God to draw close to them and to make the world grow in divine love. They will then be increasingly better able to combat confusion and injustice, and offer up their sufferings and their joys to Christ the Savior, who gives them his spirit in their daily lives.

Christians will seek to link their work, whatever it may be, to the One who speaks directly to our hearts through the mouths of all the poor.

Hunger in the Dominican Republic

It has been so interesting to follow the debate in the Dominican Republic over the UN report on hunger among children. Almost one out of three suffers some form of malnutrition. I suspect this is under reported because Haitians are usually not included in the census. Government officials over the last few days have blamed corruption for hunger. I suspect this is true because there are few controls on the export of food, especially rice, that is sold to the US for higher prices. Rice is actually imported by the DR even though it grows enough to feed its people. The poor have to buy imported rice at much higher prices. The second reason cited by government officials is that there are too many Haitians in the DR. They eat too much and therefore there is not enough food. This is an outrageous claim that only a simpleton would suggest. Even if the government official believes this theory, it should never be said because it exposes the underbelly of bigotry against Haitians in the DR who are here search for food. I know this is a complex problem, but to blame the most vulnerable and hungry for the problem of hunger is absurd.

The United Nations World Food Program (WFP) is expressing concern about the increased levels of malnutrition among the Dominican population, as reported in the Listin Diario. According to the UN the percentage of malnutrition has increased from 6.1% in 2000 to 7.2% in 2006 and more than two million Dominicans, 27% of the population, suffers from hunger. According to Pavel Isa, WFP's representative in the DR, eight out of every 100 children in the DR suffers from irreparable growth retardation due to a lack of quality nutrition. Isa said that statistics show a decrease in malnutrition during the early 90s but there has now been an increase with there being close to 20,000 additional children affected by malnutrition from 2002-2006. Isa warns that the each year 2,500 more children will be affected if action isn't taken soon. Isa also cited data from the polls ENDESA (2002 statistics) and ENHOGAR (2006 statistics), which point out that between 7% and 9% of children up to the age of three suffer from chronic malnutrition, which translates into between 56,000 and 74,000 infants with irreversible growth retardation. Isa reminded the government of its promise to cut hunger in half by 2015, as part of the UN Millennium Goals, and lamented the fact that the US$200 million investment in food programs has been "indirect and ineffective". Public Health Minister Bautista Rojas Gomez attributed the increase to mismanagement of the 2003 banking crisis by the past Mejia government

Hunger and Hate

Street kids do not get much fat in their diet. Often I will provide a treat of chicken and fries. They love it. A couple of men from Washington D.C. toured areas of poverty in Puerto Plata and we talked about the many problems here, especially the Haitian/Dominican issue. In some ways Americans relate to this through our exposure to the Mexican American border issues. What is our obligation to our brother and sister, regardless of nationality, skin color, and station in life. We have all these artificial divisions based on nationality, social class, and political borders and we use them as reasons to not help or serve our brother and sister in need. We see this all the time in the news were people say that Mexicans should not have access to medical services in US hospitals even if it is an emergency. I read about people in the DR who complain that Haitians access Dominican medical services.

I know these are large and complicated problems that require broad strategic answers. On the most fundamental level we must address these issues because there are answers to them. For example, in Africa where the biggest medical problem is HIV there are enormous disparities is the rate of disease. 28% of the people in South Africa are infected but in Senegal less than 1%. There are pockets of hope where prevention is actually working. The same can be done when tackling the problems of hunger, poverty, or homelessness. It is a matter of moral will.

Hunger Eradication: It takes only one!

Recently woman came to me and was full of joy and sorrow. I had talked to her a few days before and I told her of the plight of the Haitians in the Dominican Republic. It flew right over her head. The next day she went to the border to hand out candy. She caused a riot. Children scratched her and were stepping on one another. She saw the desperation. As the bus was ready to leave a hundred women gathered around begging for a dollar. One woman haunted her last night. She could not sleep. She knows this child the woman was carrying was dying because of hunger. She thought of staying an extra day, paying a hundred extra dollars to return and give this woman twenty dollars. Then she thought of what we talked about a few days before. What good would it do to hand out money? The people will be hungry again in a few days. Why not return home, develop a program that is sustainable, and return and work with the people to give them skills and tools so they can help themselves. This was an "AH HA" moment for her. She understands what many others and we are trying to do here. Create programs, like micro credit projects that give people dignity. She will go home, talk to friends and together we will develop something through our program or another affiliate group and create something that will have long-term effects.

Here is her response:

"I am the woman who Dale was writing about. I just arrived back to New Jersey late last night and the first thing I did was email Dale so he can help me get started. I thought I had it bad raising twin girls age 25 by myself with no help from their father But I had it great. This trip has changed my life. I cannot stop thinking about the people and how I can try to help them. What a GREAT feeling and I haven't even really started except by telling people at my hotel what I plan to do. They were from all over   the U.S., England, Ireland, and Germany they all gave me email address and said they will help. My father always thought I would grow up and become a missionary and maybe this it what I can give. Thank goodness I met Dale."

Milk

In our milk program and census work we have run across a number of mothers with HIV/AIDS. Many of them are mothers of infants one and two years old. Some of them are entering the stages of AIDS. I have talked to one women in particular for a number of months. She is so hard, angry, and sad. But yesterday I saw somewhat of a breakthrough. For the first time I saw her smile. The day before she had a big argument with me. She wanted money of course. I told her no but that I would bring her pampers and medicine at 5 pm in the afternoon. She did not believe me as people on the street live day by day. There is no tomorrow. But I said to her that tomorrow is the future. If she would wait till tomorrow then I would give her what she and her child need. She walked away cursing me. Of course the next day a five in the afternoon after distributing medicine, milk, and pampers to other HIV/AIDS mothers I waited at the appointed location for this mother. She was not there. Nevertheless, I waited another 15 minutes and finally she showed up. She was so happy and ran up and hugged me. I could see there was a breakthrough in my relationship to her and I think it will have impact on the other mothers as well.

What is really sad is that the national health plan, such as it is in the Dominican Republic, does not cover HIV/AIDS care. While on the local level we may be impacting a few lives, on the national level, this problem needs to be addressed.

Hunger and Human Development

On almost a daily basis I see the relationship between hunger and development. In my blog I wrote:

"It was a near perfect day. We passed out school supplies (Thanks to Dave from Canada) including pens, paper, and crayons. We visited women very ill from HIV/AIDS and unable to care for their children. We testing children's reading skills, and we gave more rice and beans to our feeding center. In return we got hugs from kids, recognition from people on the street, and a chance to thank the many people who are helping to feed and educate these children. It is a team effort and a portrait of human hearts responding to the needs of others."

"Sometimes we wonder if we are making any progress in the DR. Yesterday we took a group of Canadians to see our school project in Congrejo. Fifteen new rooms are being added to the previous five we worked on last spring and summer. Senior Srauss, Senior Tejada, and the local people of Congrejo, and all our volunteers have joined together to keep this project moving. We originally projected a school of 300 students but 600 showed up. With the additional rooms there will be enough space. If you want to work on a school project in the DR we will need volunteers to help paint, bring school supplies, and help teach. If education is your mission then this little school could use your help. Last year they were sitting under trees and under tin roofs. This year they have a building. It is the best way to change a society in the long term.

Sometimes the corruption and various difficulties of trying to get things done here discourage us. But here is a shinning example that there is hope for the future of these children and their country that we love so much."

Serve the Poor

> Increasingly, the great cities of the world "are mega cities infected by a social cancer, magnets pulling people to them, whirlpools sucking people into a bottomless vortex of misery. They are a blend of slum pollution, poverty, crime, corruption."
>
> - R. Franklin Cook, editor of *World Mission*

Over the past 100 years, on every populated continent of the world, people have been leaving rural areas in record numbers and seeking refuge in the city. For the first time in history, more than half of the world's population now lives in cities. Instead of finding refuge, however, many of these people find misery. More than 31 percent of the people living in the world's 50 largest cities are poor, powerless, and dying in urban slums - and the numbers are increasing.

We're seeing the greatest migration of people in human history, a migration of hemispheric proportion. More than 30 million people are wandering around the world without a home - and over half of them are Africans migrating in search of bread. The cities are the catch basins of these folks. The frontier of world mission is no longer geographically distant. It's culturally distant and geographically right next-door. It reminds me of Psalm 107, which is filled with images of people looking for a city to dwell in. In the Bible the city was a place of hope. If we really start reading Psalm 107 and other scriptures again, we'll gain a whole new perspective on what our cities need to look like as the catch basins of hope.

In Madras, India, for example - a city with over 8 million people and something like 1,000 slums -- World Vision is working in five slums, organizing churches and mission's agencies and nongovernmental organizations to work together with the people. In five years, World Vision invested $34,000 in bringing these groups together. The result was, we got the government to build 2,000 homes, to deed land to 2,000 poor families, to build and open three schools and a library, to install adequate public toilets, to asphalt roads, and to put in street lighting, house wiring, and sewer lines -- which cost the government $1.5 million. So $34,000 was leveraged into $1.5 million.

The point is not to focus on the needs of poor communities, but to see their capacities and begin to work from strength. The $1.5 million and the government's capacity to use it was there all the time

Different Kinds of Poverty

I have been thinking a lot lately about poverty. What is poverty? It seems like there are at least three kinds. The first kind is derived from pity and envy. The poor envy the rich and suffer because of their desire for more. The rich often pity the poor and transfer a kind of arrogance by valuing a person based on how much "stuff" he or she possesses. This is why I do not like people giving our program money for us to use to serve others and they themselves do not serve with us.

This is why I believe people should volunteer and directly assist the poor. This is not an option according to the Bible I read, it is an obligation.

The second kind of poverty is a poverty of resources where a person simply does not have enough to live. There isn't enough food, medicine, clean water, shelter, or clothing to stay alive. This is the kind of abject poverty that politicians recently have been talking about eliminating.

The third kind of poverty is a poverty of spirit. "Blessed are the poor in spirit" Jesus said. This is a deeply mystical and profound idea. It means emptying ourselves of ego and attachment to things. It means being liberated from "stuff" and dispossessing ourselves from envy and pity. When that happens we become poor in spirit. I see this happen in the volunteers who work with us. The very act of serving the poor transforms pity into compassion.

On the other hand, poverty reduces people to selling their bodies.

Poverty and Sexual Abuse

On this Caribbean country's white beaches, teenage and child prostitutes wearing next to nothing troll the resort areas, frolicking near groups of foreign tourists to lure their attention away from the emerald seas. Poorly educated and immersed in poverty, they offer themselves for pennies — a desperate act that activists say is helping spread the AIDS virus in the country.

"I do it for the money," said a lanky 16-year-old boy who gave his name as Eduardo. "I don't need to get tested because I know I'm not sick."

Like dozens of others, he walks the Puerto Plata beachfront, 100 miles northwest of the capital Santo Domingo, shining shoes and occasionally selling himself to the highest bidder.

At least 35,000 Dominican youths under 19 have turned to prostitution for survival, and as many as 15 percent of them could be HIV positive, according to Mais, a Dominican non-governmental organization working to end child prostitution in the Spanish-speaking country.

The Dominican government estimates that at least 130,000 Dominicans have HIV, the virus that leads to AIDS, and more than 52,000 have died from the disease since 1985. Unlike adult prostitutes who often work at nightclubs and are required to be tested for HIV and other sexually transmitted diseases, child prostitutes are largely unregulated.

"I always use a condom, but many don't and I know of many who have (AIDS)," says 17-year-old Jose Luis, who earns between 400 and 500 pesos per hour, about $20-25, working as a prostitute. He supplements his income by feeding chickens at a local farm. He said a friend told him he could earn a lot of money in the resort town of Cabarete, about 25 miles from Puerto Plata. But he now has to share part of his profits with a pimp who leaves him notes at a local hotel informing him of his next trick.

Less than half of child prostitutes use condoms regularly, and only 38 percent have been tested for AIDS, says an October study by Profamilia, a Dominican family planning organization. In July and August 2001, the group surveyed 118 prostitutes between ages 10 and 17 in Puerto Plata and Santo Domingo.

Profamilia and Mais say many parents know their children are prostitutes, but in some cases the families encourage it to ease their crushing poverty. The country has been known for years as a sex tourism destination.

"In some nightclubs one can find brochures with pictures of naked children and phone numbers for taxi drivers that will take them to child prostitutes," said Maria Josefina Paulino of Mais.

Janet, a 17-year-old prostitute who is pregnant with triplets, said she was forced into the trade at 13 when she had a son and couldn't feed him. She has worked in the Puerto Plata beachfront for the last four years.

"I started sneaking out my house to do it," she said. "I left my house when I was 14."

Janet was tested for AIDS a week ago because of her pregnancy, and the results came out negative. "I know AIDS kills because a friend of mine died from that, so I always use a condom," she said.

Her 26-year-old friend Mariluz began prostituting herself when she was 14. When she was 16 she worked in a nightclub where the owners made her use a condom and get tested for HIV.

Social taboos and scant resources for education mean many children don't understand the risks. Some groups say to educate child prostitutes on the use of condoms and the dangers of AIDS would essentially be endorsing the trade.

"The country has a series of weaknesses in protecting its children, including protection against AIDS," says Jaime de la Rosa, joint director of the government AIDS council.

In the meantime, Mais and Profamilia fear the virus will continue to advance without a nationwide education campaign directed at child prostitutes.

Profamilia and MAIS say many parents know their children are prostitutes, but in some cases the families encourage it to ease their crushing poverty. The country has been known for years as a sex tourism destination. "In some nightclubs one can find brochures with pictures of naked children and phone numbers for taxi drivers that will take them to child prostitutes," said Maria Josefina Paulino of MAIS.

MAIS (Movimiento Para el Autodesarrollo Internacional de la Solidaridad) is a non-profit organization, founded in 1998 in Puerta Plata, Dominican Republic. MAIS administered care to 68 children in high-risk situations (children who are out of school, or in school but doing poorly, victims of sexual abuse or those who have experienced commercial sexual exploitation); and dealt with 39 cases of sexual violence against children and 6 cases of sexual exploitation of children of a commercial nature.

For 13-year-old Elvia, life in the Dominican Republic's resort town of Puerto Plata is hardly a vacation. Since her parents separated, Elvia's mother has chosen to settle with her new husband and two young sons. Elvia must live with her grandmother who, as a single older woman, is hard-pressed to make ends meet. At such a young age, Elvia, along with hundreds of other impoverished children in her community, must make a difficult choice between pursuing her education or earning a living in order to support herself. Sadly, with little incentive or encouragement to stay in poorly-funded schools and few legitimate opportunities to earn money, girls such as Elvia are easily lured into Puerto Plata's lucrative sex tourism industry. Defenseless to the physical and sexual abuse that so often accompanies prostitution, these young children find themselves in one of the most vulnerable and exploited groups of Puerto Plata's society.

Fortunately for Elvia, the community-based organization MAIS (translated into English as International Solidarity Self-Development Movement) has provided her with an alternative to the commercial sex trade. Founded in 1998, MAIS strives to motivate children to stay in school and to prevent initial or continued sexual exploitation by offering academic support and social services to at-risk and exploited youth. Operating on an annual budget equivalent to $28,000, MAIS focuses on preventative work, providing children with the skills and confidence that allow them to create social opportunities for themselves without resorting to prostitution. Although the young people who participate in MAIS are not usually former sex workers, many of them are victims of sexual and physical abuse inflicted at home or on the streets.

Training for Life community center is a supplementary school program that serves sixty-two boys and girls in the Limonera neighborhood of Puerto Plata. These children and young teens attend classes at MAIS three times a week either before or after their part-time formal school day. In addition to instruction in core curriculum subjects such as writing, reading, mathematics, and science, the children participate in workshops on human rights and the special rights of children and can take advantage of vocational and craft workshops. The MAIS staff works closely with the children's families and teachers in an effort to reinforce the value of staying in school and pursuing productive opportunities in life. Elvia, who has participated in MAISs program for more than a year, proudly says that she has learned much in the academic areas of math, history, and science, but more importantly, Elvia reports; I have learned how to depend and take care of myself.

MAIS is part of the worldwide ECPAT (Ending Child Prostitution, Pornography and Trafficking) network. With members in more than fifty countries, ECPAT advocates for the elimination child prostitution, child sex tourism, child pornography, and trafficking of children for sexual purposes.

Elvia, along with hundreds of other impoverished children in her community, must make a difficult choice between pursuing her education or earning a living in order to support herself. Sadly, with little incentive or encouragement to stay in poorly funded schools and few legitimate opportunities to earn money, girls such as Elvia are easily lured into Puerto Plata's lucrative sex tourism industry.

Sexual exploitation of children is a problem. Some in the tourist industry have facilitated the sexual exploitation of children; particular areas of concern are Boca Chica and Puerto Plata. Tours are marketed by foreigners overseas with the understanding that boys and girls can be found as sex partners.

The Dominican Republic has ratified the International Labor Organization (ILO) Convention (105) on the Abolition of Forced Labor; the ILO Convention (182) to Eliminate the Worst Forms of Child Labor; the United Nations (UN) Supplementary Convention on the Abolition of Slavery, the Slave Trade, and Institutions and Practices Similar to Slavery; and signed the UN Protocol to Prevent, Suppress, and Punish Trafficking in Persons, Especially Women and Children.

However, the Dominican Republic has not ratified the Optional Protocol to the UN Convention on the Rights of the Child on the Sale of Children, Child Prostitution, and Child Pornography or the UN International Convention on the Protection of the Rights of All Migrant Workers and Members of Their Families.

In the Dominican Republic, there is a considerable population of minors for whom the streets have become home, who have faced a hostile world from an early age. Most "street children" beg as a means of subsistence; one-third turn to robbery and other means to get by, such as selling drugs; and approximately one-fifth engage in prostitution.

Blaming the Poor

If you ask typical Americans what percentage of the federal budget is spent on welfare, they'd probably say about 20 percent. They think we can save money in the budget by cutting back on welfare. Further, one of the basic principles in welfare reform is that you have to stop giving away so much money to people who are on welfare because they don't deserve it. The argument goes that we middle-class people have to go out and work hard for our money. Then we just give it away to poor people through programs like Aid to Dependent Children. So, the argument says, all these programs ought to be abolished.

But if welfare is eliminated, who will this affect? It's going to affect the most vulnerable people in our society. The typical person on welfare is a woman with two children who has no means of support, no capacity for income, little education, and can't get work. There are no jobs out there for a person like that. And if a job was available, it would take her away from raising her children. So she's extremely vulnerable and totally dependent on that aid.

The truth is, we won't save significant amounts of money by cutting back on welfare. In reality, less than one percent of the national budget goes for welfare. The amount of money actually spent on welfare is so minimal that it is impossible to reform it significantly without actually eliminating it as an effective tool. A 1 percent change in the federal budget is not going to profoundly affect the budget.

We have to show that poor people in the cities are not the only ones benefiting from federal aid. Electrical power is cheaper in my home state of Washington because the federal government controls the Bonneville Power Co., which controls 30 dams, and is really a subsidized electrical base that allows cheaper farming and dairy operations. But we don't call it Aid to Dependent Farmers.

Along with the explosion of technology and a rapid increase of population came the explosive growth of cities. Here are quotes taken from *World Urbanization Prospects* published by a United Nations agency in 1998:

It is projected that just after the turn of the millennium, in a few years, for the first time in history urban dwellers will outnumber those in traditional rural areas . . . By 2006, half of the world population are expected to be urban dwellers. The urban population is growing three times faster than its rural counterpart. By 2030, three of every five persons will be living in urban areas.

Implications for Christian Missions

Missions during the twenty-first century must face the fact that the majority of the world's population increasingly will be living in cities. Cities are to be the target of mission penetration not only because most ethnic groups once living in rural areas now have representatives in cities; they are to be the target also because cities contain many social groups that have not yet been reached with the gospel. Furthermore, cities are centers of dominance and therefore are the pacesetters for a society. If numerous groups in the giant cities of the world receive the gospel, the good news of God's salvation may then spread from city to hinterland just as it did in New Testament times.

"He took the disciples with him and had discussions daily in the lecture hall of Tyrannus. This went on for two years, so that all the Jews and Greeks who lived in the province of Asia heard the word of the Lord" (Acts 19:9b-10). "The Lord's message rang out from you not only in Macedonia and Achaia-your faith in God has become known everywhere" (1 Thess. 1:8).

Many cities in the Southern World (or the developing world) are growing even though they have high rates of unemployment and are surrounded by the shantytowns of the poor.

This is not a new idea in Christian circles. More than one hundred years ago, the Dutch reformer, theologian, and statesman, Abraham Kuyper said:

> The gospel speaks to you of a Redeemer who, although he was rich, became poor for your sake so he might make you rich.
>
> It points you to God's Son, but one who became the Son of Man and went through the country, from wealthy Judea to the poorer, despised Galilee, addressing himself to those who were in need or oppressed by sorrow. Yes, it tells

you that this singular Savior, before he left
this earth, stooped before his disciples in
the clothes of a slave, washed their feet
one by one, and then stood and said,
"For I have given you an example, that
ye should do as I have done to you"
(John 13:15).

Remembering the poor in the giant cities of the
world is not to suggest that only the giant cities ought
to receive our attention. It has already been observed
that if one looks at sheer numbers, the majority of
urban residents actually live in much smaller cities,
and the smaller cities are also important.

Then the Lord said, "Broadcast this message in
Jerusalem's streets. Go from city to city throughout
the land" (Jeremiah 7 1:6).

Education: the way out of poverty

There is interesting research to show that education
is the most fundamental way to combat poverty. What
is interesting is to note the kind of education that is
most effective. Current global research shows that
PUBLIC education is the best method. PRIVATE
schools actually reinforce the problems of poverty.
Unless there is universal access to education the rich
get richer and the classes remain divided. This is way
to measure educational success, as a way to combat
poverty is to monitor the decline in *colleges*, private
schools and the rise of public schools. Private schools
only reinforce the status of the elite, drain vital human
resources, and keep the poor in their place.

Illiteracy is one of the strongest predictors of poverty, and unequal access to educational opportunity correlates strongly with income inequality. The case for 'education for all', of course, goes beyond these economic arguments. Education helps provide 'human capabilities', the 'essential and individual power to reflect, make choices, seek a voice in society, and enjoy a better life' (Sen, 1999).

In developing countries, however, there are huge disparities in the levels of education achieved by young people. The average years of schooling completed is only 3.52 in sub-Saharan Africa, and 4.57 in South Asia, the two lowest regions. Recognizing the seriousness of these problems, at the Dakar Forum in 2000, 189 countries committed themselves to eradicating poverty and improving people's welfare, through, amongst others, achieving universal primary education by 2015.

Government intervention the assumed solution

The problem of low levels of education is uncontroversial; and the desire of countries to achieve universal primary education is to be applauded. However, it also seems more or less universally accepted in development circles that it is a matter for *governments and bilateral and multilateral agencies* to solve this problem of achieving education for all. For instance, in the latest World Bank deliberations on the education targets (World Bank, 2002, p. 44), the estimate is that reaching them will take $13 billion a year until 2015, the vast majority of which must be supplied by international agencies and administered through governments.

Perhaps this assumption will seem uncontroversial to some readers too, that it has to be through government action, supported by international agencies, that educational aims for the poor can be achieved. But, reading the small print of the World Bank report, an interesting peculiarity emerges, that throws a different light on the problem. The authors note that in many of the countries that require the most assistance, *private sector* enrolments in primary education exceed their desired target of 10% (arrived at by noting what the "most successful" developing countries achieve). In India, for instance, it is 27% of all enrolments. Such levels are only there because of 'the limited supply or poor quality of public schooling'. But since they envisage 'quality improvement and expansion' in *public* schools, in such countries enrolment in private schools must decline progressively to below 10%. Such a *decline* in private sector enrolments they argue is 'an efficiency gain'.

In other words, it is assumed in the most recent World Bank report on the subject – sentiments echoed throughout by development policy makers – that private education in developing countries is undesirable, so much so that any successful policy must inevitably lead to its decline as a proportion of the whole. Certainly private education is not seen as a valuable agent in the drive for 'education for all'. The report's authors do seek to justify this position: 'the attainment of universal primary completion is a responsibility of national governments', and because the very poorest can't afford private schools, 'therefore' the vast majority should not be allowed to make such choices either.

Education

Marta and I had the honor of hosting Dr. David Penney and his partner. Dr. Penney is a specialist in spiders and recently discovered a new spider in amber at the Amber Museum in Puerto Plata. *Missionella Didicosta* is the name of this spider. I took Dr. Penney and his wife to Ascension Village for a day and we collected spiders with the children of the village. We caught a lot of spiders. The children were quite knowledgeable about the locations of these spiders. I do not think we would have caught as many unless they had helped us. Dr. Penney was quite sure we found some new species. He will know for sure when he gets back to his laboratory at the University of Manchester in England. Dr. Penney and his companion Zen said it was the best day they had in the Dominican Republic. Inspiring children to do science is a heartwarming experience. Dr. Penney hopes to come back and do more research. His companion hopes to spend her time volunteering among the children. They are testimony to the intuitive knowledge that real service to the poor is through education.

Poverty and Jail

Over the last year we have had to go to the police station to get children in our feeding program out of jail. Periodically they round up street kids as young as 5 years old and put them in a holding room without water or food for an entire day. I ask the police why they do this to the children. They tell me that the tourists complain that the kids are harassing them. I have never heard a tourist complain yet. I have wondered what other motives there might be for this blatantly illegal act by the police. Today I read a report by the International Women's Rights Watch that an 85-year-old woman was jailed in Barahona and used as bait to attract her family members so the police could deport them to Haiti. Of course what happens is that the family payoff the police not to deport them and that is the end of it. The report goes on to says how it is a common practice to use innocent children as bait. This is sheer laziness and outright criminality on the part of police in regard to international law. Lately the police have been good about feeding and hydrating the children. They have taken them to one of our feeding centers, or at least let them out so they can get fed. The more we live here and work among the poor and homeless, the more we understand the difficulties the poor face on a daily basis. It makes us want to do even more.

Models of Mission

Two assumptions in mission seem self-evident. The first is that Jesus is our model for mission. Did he not say, "As the Father has sent me even so I send you" (John 20:21)? And did not his first declaration of his own great commission tell us:

> The Spirit of the Lord is upon me, because he has anointed me to preach good news to the poor. He has sent me to proclaim release to the captives and recovering of sight to the blind, to set at liberty those who are oppressed, to

proclaim the acceptable year of the Lord (Luke
4:18-19).

Surely with these words he modeled the gospel as
primarily good news for the poor. And he defined
ministry to the poor, declaring that the ministry to the
poor is holistic, involving preaching, healing,
deliverance, justice and doing good deeds, but is
initiated by proclamation of the kingdom.

The second set of assumptions is simply pragmatic
missionary strategizing:

1. Urban is the direction of history.

2. The poor are the direction of responsiveness. This is
true both in Jesus' teaching and in mission history as
well as sociological analysis.

3. The migrant poor are the greatest responsive group
across the face of the earth today. I have found this
responsiveness among Muslims in Iraq, Hindus in
Calcutta, Buddhists in Thailand, and Catholics in
Manila. All are in a state of rapid socioeconomic and
worldview change and are hungry for meaning.

Jesus commands a focus not so much on the
unresponsive people groups in the world, but on
responsive. The period of time within five years of a
person's or family's migration is one of those times of
greatest responsiveness.

Dr. Roger Greenway, who has done a great deal to
focus people's attention on urban missions, speaks of
his ministry to the urban poor with the phrase: "If the
streets are paved, move on."

The experience of walking through the slums and seeing hundreds of thousands of squatters in destitute poverty is devastating. As history moves towards its climax, the wound in God's heart for this migration of people must make it difficult for him to hold back his judgment. To walk again and again into the destitution of these millions sears the soul with a darkness and grotesqueness that we could not cope with outside of the rest of Christ that comes from the refreshing balm of his Spirit and the hope of the returning King.

If the destitution of the urban poor is staggering in itself, their numerical growth is just as devastating. Since World War II, an endless convoy of smoke-belching, over laden, chicken-squawking bus after bus have careened down newly-constructed highways into the mega-city capitals of the Third World, disgorging crowds of wide-eyed impoverished farmers and teenagers looking for the next step towards affluence (or, more likely, poverty) in the squatter areas.

Wherever land can be found, huts and shacks go up. Few governments have the capacity to prevent it or to provide services for the people arriving. The majority of new arrivals remain in squatter areas. Each capital city will continue to grow exponentially as it exploits the resources of its rural hinterland.

Hardly a church, rarely a pastor, seldom a missionary

More nightmarish than the poverty and the staggering growth of that poverty is to find no more than a handful of God's men, God's women ministering among these poor in each city.

I do not mean that there are no relief and development agencies. They are many, and most of them are doing good work in their roles as diaconal agencies of the church. *But the church has given bread to the poor and has kept the bread of life for the middle class.*

My search for missional solutions has not been for aid programs but for people who are establishing the kingdom of God, for the men and women working and living among the poor to bring them the bread of life by both word and deed.

I have found only a few. In the midst of the darkness, they are some of today's heroes. In each city, a handful of people have followed Jesus fully in his calls to renunciation and involvement with the poor.

There is a pastor in one west Singapore who wears the sandals and blanket of the poor, walking as holy men do. God has used him to mobilize and deploy 300 workers into the slums.

There is a man of God, a doctor, on the streets of Indonisia ministering to the sick. The government has tried to deport him for ministering to the poor. For four years he has remained, by bringing a court case against the government and quietly continuing to serve the poor.

There is a pastor who for some years has chosen to live among the poor in a relocation area of Manila. He has worked to provide housing for the poorest in his community. The official housing manager and gang leaders were curious about this man and his concern for their people. They decided to help him build houses. Ultimately, they were converted because of his obedience in living out the love and justice of God among them.

There is excitement in Bangkok, for a new generation of creative church leaders is seeing new breakthroughs for the gospel. There are now 97 churches in this city of nearly six million.

Hidden in these statistics is an old, highly successful Finnish Pentecostal church planter. At the age of 70, he daily spends long hours in a slum area, quietly establishing a church.

Despite all of this, there are only two churches and two house groups in Bangkok's 1,024 slums. Only two percent of churches are among the migrant poor.

Examples of men and women who are following Jesus in his ministry to the poor should not be the exception but the rule, if we as a church were truly following Jesus. We must refocus our energies and make the urban poor the primary thrust of missions.

The great mistakes serving the poor

When faced with the sad failure of the great mission thrust to reach these poor one must ask "why?" and beyond the why, "What can be done to rectify this failure?" The following appear to be some factors:

1. As mission leaders we have failed to foresee both the immensity of urban growth and the fact that most of the urban growth would be in squatter areas. The opportunity to save the cities from many traumas associated with this development, as well as the opportunity to establish a church in every squatter area that has formed have been lost almost entirely.

Perhaps it is because these poor are hidden. As we drive through third-world cities we see occasional glimpses of squatter and slum communities, but they are tucked behind houses and buildings and down in the hollows by the river, so that no one sees them. Those who emerge are dressed in their best clothes, soon to blend in with the middle-class people of the city. No one knows that they are poor. The poor do not advertise their misfortune.

2. Some missions have made a deliberate attempt to reach the rich, believing in a sort of religious "trickle-down" theory. "Trickle-down" works no more in the kingdom than it does in the economic realm. This strategic mistake lacks support both in biblical exegesis and in sociological analysis, and already has been competently refuted.

The gospel "trickles up." Any man or woman who would follow Jesus and walk among the poor will affect countless members of the middle and rich classes. People in these classes will come to the slums because they are curious. They hear of good deeds and like Nicodemus, they come seeking for truth and reality.

Despite the failure of affluent missionaries to preach the words of Scripture about unjust wealth and to live simply themselves, the converted rich come because these new believers can read the Bible. They come searching for the person who has chosen the poor, because they know that here is a true answer to the problems of wealth. They come because they are now concerned for the uplift of those they previously exploited. Jesus has an answer for the rich man. The rich middle-class missionary often has only words.

3. The same strategic reasons that led to defeat for an affluent power in the Vietnam War have led to failure in this spiritual war. Depending on affluent and high-powered programmatic approaches, the mission force has been out of touch with the realities of the third-world poor. A missionary living on $2800 per month in a western-style house and sending his children to a westerners' school while trying to reach people who live on $200 per year is an insult to the Jesus they think they serve.

4. This failure in the great Western mission thrust is, at its roots, ultimately not strategic but spiritual. A church trapped by cultural perspectives on affluence rather than adopting the biblical stance of opposition to the "god of mammon" has exported this into missions. We must return to the pattern of Jesus, who chose non-destitute poverty as a way of life, took the time to learn language and culture, and refused to be a welfare agency king. We must return to the way of the apostles and of the wandering friars who have been the key to the conversion of the world in generations before us. Non-destitute poverty and simplicity must again become focal in mission strategy.

5. Some perhaps have concluded that the poor are unreachable. This is a culturally logical conclusion for those of European descent growing up in the capitalism of the United States.:

The poverty of the third-world urban poor, however, is a direct result of social forces and oppression, not of personal sin. The oppressed poor in the Scriptures are considered to be rich in faith and the ones for whom the kingdom is particularly to be preached.

6. The propensity for the Western church to accept the agenda of aid organizations as focal to the Great Commission has seriously skewed mission. Mission to the middle class is seen as proclamation. To the poor it has become giving handouts or assisting in development as defined by Christianized humanitarian perspectives. It is far easier for churches to give thousands of dollars than to find one of their members who will walk into the slums for a decade.

New Monasticism

My convictions have deepened and been modified during my years of wandering, preaching and living among the poor.

The central one remains: we must thrust out groups similar to the devotional communities of 12th century preaching friars, or the wandering Irish monks that converted Northern Europe between the fifth and ninth centuries, before the Catholic hierarchy gained control there. In our case we must send communities of men and women, married couples and singles, with commitments to live as the poor among the poor in order to preach the kingdom and establish the church in these great slum areas.

Westerners and upper-class nationals who choose such lives of non-destitute poverty may be catalysts for movements of lay leaders from among the poor in each city. The spearhead of such a thrust will be those who accept the gift of singleness for some years. We must set up new mission structures for this to happen. The key is young couples who will choose to give leadership to these communities of pioneers.

We need men and women who will commit themselves to lives of simplicity, poverty, devotion, community, and sacrifice in areas of marriage and family.

Most missionary teams are not communities, but teams of individuals, often selfish and self centered. See what I did for Jesus is their theme. The focus of most of these pseudo-teams is to work building schools and churches and avoiding real relationships with the poor.

Poverty, chastity, obedience

The commitments to non-destitute poverty may be similar to those of the older Catholic orders, without the legalism.

So too is a commitment to singleness - taken not as a vow of celibacy, but for a period of time. Protestants have lost the concept of the gift of singleness. Marriage has been seen as the only ideal. The biblical blessing on chosen or given singleness has to be recovered. Part of the blessing of that gift is freedom to pioneer in difficult and dangerous places.

Obedience for Protestants is democratized by the emphasis on the priesthood of all believers.

New structures

Historically, movements among the poor have consistently been thrown out of the middle-class churches. It would be wise for mission directors to create new orders of men and women called to the poor. These could be within or without their old mission boards.

Such orders should only be guided by persons in authority who have lived, for long periods, this kind of sacrificial and incarnational lifestyle. Authority should never be given to administrators who have not lived out this lifestyle. Incarnational workers do not want protection. They want pastoral care from leaders who have been on the front line, who will keep them at the front line, and who will take the "bullets" out when the workers are wounded.

An Incarnational Call

The need is urgent for several thousand men and women to live in the slums of third-world cities who can generate transformations in each city. To live in solidarity with the poor to the real expression of the Gospel. Two billion people cry out.

I believe God will not leave their cries unheard.

The Face of Poverty

In the northern hemisphere, the urban poor live predominantly within inner cities. In the southern hemisphere, they cluster mainly around the cities. Most of those in the northern hemisphere would be classified as relatively poor, whereas almost all in the southern hemisphere are absolutely poor. Despite many differences in the groupings of the poor, the Brandt Report and research by UNA and the WHO clearly indicate that urban poor worldwide have in common:

- feelings of powerlessness, insignificance, frustration, and despair
- fearfulness of the future
- low health expectation
- inadequate housing
- unemployment or underemployment
- insufficient money
- poor provision for education
- a higher rate of crime
- political turmoil

There are large, long-established reservoirs of the poor in the inner cities of Europe and North America; floods of work-seeking rural dwellers pouring into the cities of Latin America, Asia, and Africa; increasing streams of refugees from natural disaster and political repression. The urban poor are to be found in the CALLAMPAS (mushroom cities) of Chile, the BUSTEES of India, the GOURBEVILLES of Tunisia, the SECEKINDU (built after dusk and before dawn) of Turkey, the GHETTOS of the U.S.A., and the SLUMS of Australia. Such settlements are often a third to a half of the urban population.

The urban poor are a fast-growing, harsh reality. Despite political initiatives and concerned social action, urban poverty appears to be intractable. The situation has not been helped by the relief policies, in which so much hope has been placed. The gap between the rich northern hemisphere and the poor southern hemisphere is widening—while 25% live in unprecedented affluence, 75% are trapped in poverty. The disparity between the rich and the poor within the countries of the northern hemisphere exists and is widening. There is an apparent determinism of economic laws, which perpetuates the problems of the urban poor.

The church as a whole is trapped in an ignorance about the urban poor, the causes and consequences of their poverty, and the extent and gravity of our complicity in it.

From India:

The migrants who have come in from the village are easily exploited, live in the worst housing slums, are unorganized, and, if they find work, provide the dirty services from which others benefit. They have no skills because of the break, made by coming to the city, with their traditional rural skills. For these people, their rural and feudal background determines everything. They come to their own relatives, their own caste and language groups, with which they have ties. These provide no security for them. Unless they can find a job in a few days, they are thrown out of their homes. The major concern is survival. They have little time for anything else. However horrific the national figures for deprivation in India are, they will be higher among this group. So while illiteracy nationally stands at 90%, among this group it will be 90-100%. They lack everything.

In LATIN AMERICA, rural dwellers have been pushing into metropolitan areas since the 1930s. Fifty-five percent of the population lives around the cities in great urban conglomerations. Whole families come with expectations of work and money, but their hope soon becomes despair. Cities are unable to provide basic facilities, and employment is menial and often supplemented by begging and prostitution. Mere subsistence (10 in a one-room house) brings resignation or revolution.

In AFRICA, the peoples of central and eastern Africa are drawn to the cities by the lure of higher pay. They become de-tribalised and lose the taboos and constraints as their sense of belonging is eroded. Their numbers are being augmented by refugees fleeing oppression or driven by famine. In South Africa, urban blacks provide the labor force. Huge townships like Soweto part husband from wife. Voiceless and powerless, they neither belong to the white-dominated cities nor the homesteads they occupy. In African cities there are 60 million unemployed male adults and many others under-employed.

In ASIA, people are driven to cities for survival. With no available housing, they congregate with friends or families in the slums. Suffering from malnutrition, lacking education, ignorant of their rights, lapsing into fatalism, they become trapped in the vicious cycle of poverty. So we have the exploited migrants in Calcutta without skills or organization, and the families of Hong Kong requiring two or three incomes for survival, and the young people of Bangkok drawing money from prostitution.

In AUSTRALIA, unexpected poverty juts out. Lacking the deep-rooted industrial history of Europe, or the mass rural migration of Asia, this new continent of 14 million people has "over 2 million Australians living in various degrees of poverty . . . powerless . . . voiceless and unorganized" (Australians in Poverty, Peter Hollingsworth, 1979). Here the poor are identified as pensioners, unemployed, broken families, single parents, migrant families from Eastern Europe and refugees from Asia—added to the dispossessed aboriginals.

In EUROPE, beneath the obvious poverty of the very old, the chronically unemployed, and inadequate people—lies the deeper victimization of redundancy, and a pervading sense of powerlessness. France has three million North African migrant workers drawn from Algeria, Morocco, and Tunisia. They are part of Europe's 10 million "guest workers" imported in the 1960s from the poorer part of the Mediterranean, from Black Africa, and former colonies in Asia and the Caribbean. They live alongside the long- established working classes. Groups of prostitutes, drug-dependents, vagrants, and delinquents tend to gather in the areas of the urban poor.

In NORTH AMERICA, one estimate indicates that 40/45 million Americans are within the ranks of the urban poor. Black people in the city centers, driven northwards by the revolution in Southern agriculture and lack of work opportunities, face discrimination and live in frustration. Migrant Hispanics suffer all the disadvantages of the black population with the added problem of language. Native Indians live alongside the undocumented aliens seeking anonymity, the abandoned elderly, the incoming refugees (from Laos, Kampuchea, Vietnam, Haiti, and Cuba) and the transients (alcoholics, single men, and seasonal workers). The lack of jobs, the collapse of the low-rent housing market and the cutback of public welfare services lead to a culture of despair.

And Yet!

Over against the overwhelming statistics and often appalling suffering of the urban poor, we have to set another side. Enormous reserves of creative energy are to be found among the oppressed poor. Social organization, use of personal abilities, family togetherness, and industry are often combined to create a strong inter-dependency of living. Cultural values are carried and maintained and distinctive notes of dialect, music and beliefs characterize many urban poor groups. Within them there is an impetus for change, which has powerful roots, and searches for the political machinery to effect structural revolution.

In the Old Testament, "poor" can be translated by six major and three other terms—totaling about 300 references, and revealing a broad understanding of the causes, reality, and consequences of poverty. The poor person is the downtrodden, humiliated, oppressed; the man pleading and crying out for justice; the weak or helpless; the destitute; the needy, dependent person; and the one forcibly subjected to the powerful oppressor. The wide range of terms shows that "the poor" must be seen from many perspectives. Clustering around "the poor" are linked words like "the widow," "the fatherless" and "the stranger."

The New Testament uses a number of terms to describe the poor: the manual worker who struggles to survive on a day-to-day basis, the destitute cowering as a beggar, the one reduced to "meekness," the one brought low. We must include those weak and exhausted by heavy burdens and the leper, the widows and "the common people."

Throughout the Bible the majority of references indicate that the poor are the mercilessly oppressed, the powerless, the destitute, and the downtrodden. Nor is their poverty taken for granted in Scripture. It causes concern, anger, and protest. It is challenged and opposed. And its source is seen as injustice and oppression by the powerful. God's words about the poor have been to us like rocks in an avalanche. It is possible to duck the first few, but the massive thrust is inescapable. We urge others to study for themselves, using the concordances in the appendix, or reading some of the recent books on the subject.

We have discovered that when Jesus said, "The poor you always have with you" (Mark 14:7), he was pointing out that we are sinful in permitting poverty. For his allusion is to Deut. 15:4, 5: "There will be no poor among you if only you will obey the voice of the Lord."

Jesus and the Poor

Born in a stable of humble parents and a refugee in early childhood, Jesus grew up in the despised town of Nazareth. In middle life he abandoned his craft to begin the messianic mission of good news about the unbreaking of God's kingly reign, journeying throughout Palestine, often with no place to sleep. After a brief ministry, he was put to death by the power elite of the day, crucified among criminals.

The central feature of his teaching was that in him, in his words and works, the kingly reign of God had broken into human history. Demonstrating that God's absolute future was already breaking into the present, Jesus healed the sick and exorcised demons, challenged the Sabbath regulations and predicted the end of the Temple, abolished the rigid food laws and associated with the nobodies of society, pronounced God's blessing on the poor and demonstrated his presence with the persecuted, declared the forgiveness of sins, and invited the outcasts and notorious to the kingdom banquet. All, without exception, were invited, and all, without distinction, were welcome— for this was to be a festival of grace and joy, a festival celebrating God's reign of grace.

The ministry of Jesus was open to all. He accepted the invitation to eat with the Pharisees (Luke 11:37)— but sharply denounced them; healed the daughter of the president of the synagogue (Luke 8:41) and the son of a centurion (Matthew 8:5); was supported by wealthy women (Luke 8:2-3); and was buried in the tomb of Joseph of Arimathea, a respected member of the Sanhedrin (Mark 15:42-47). The distinctive feature of his ministry, however, was that, while it was open to all, it was directed primarily towards those whom the orthodox and powerful regarded as beyond the fringes of respectability, outside the realm of salvation according to the traditions of his day. These included lepers, who had to live outside the camp (Luke 17:11-19); Gentiles who had no share in the privileges of Israel (Matthew 8:5-13; John 4:45-54); women and children who had no rights or status within the community (Matthew 9:20-26); notorious sinners, despised tax collectors, drunkards and prostitutes (Matthew 11:9; 21:32; Mark 2:16,17; Luke 7:33-50; 15:1,2; 19:1, 2).

Right at the beginning of his ministry Jesus declared in the synagogue of Nazareth that the words of the ancient prophet had come to fulfillment:

"The Spirit of the Lord is upon me, because he has chosen me to bring good news to the poor. He has sent me to proclaim liberty to the captives and recovery of sight to the blind; to set free the oppressed and announce that the time has come when the Lord will save his people" (Luke 4:18-19).

In his teaching on hospitality, Jesus commanded a host to invite "the poor, the crippled, the blind and the lame" (Luke 14:13). In the parable of the great feast,

106

the host orders his servants to go out and bring back "the poor, the crippled, the blind and the lame" (Luke 14:21) for all the invited guests had declined the invitation.

Many of his parables carried this free offer of salvation to despised outcasts and notorious sinners. They include the parable of the laborers in the vineyard (Matthew 20:1- 15); the two sons (Matthew 20:20-24); the two debtors (Luke 7:41-43); the prodigal son (Luke 15:11-32); the lost sheep (Luke 15:4-7); the lost coin (Luke 15:8-10) and the Pharisee and the publican (Luke 18:9-14).

When John the Baptist was imprisoned and wanted to be sure of the authenticity—of the messianic ministry of Jesus, he was told, "The blind can see, the lame can walk, those who suffer from dreaded skin diseases are made clean, the deaf hear, the dead are brought back to life, and the good news is preached to the poor" (Matthew 11:5, 6).

The Kingdom-Community and the Poor

The whole of the teaching of Jesus about kingdom has been increasingly recognized to be closely related to the new Israel, which Jesus called into being. The twelve disciples and those around them were the nucleus of a kingdom community, which the Messiah was to raise up. The kingdom is embodied in a new social reality, which lives in the power of the Spirit. The central theme of the new household of God, which Jesus inaugurated, was grace. Forgiveness and forgivingness, acceptance and openness, and an undiscriminating love like that of God were to be its hallmark (Matthew 5:43-48; Luke 6:27-36). Here the least would be the greatest, the servant the ruler of all, in startling contrast with a society conformed to this world.

At Pentecost, the New Testament church was empowered by the Spirit to witness to the kingdom (Luke 1:16-18), and to be anticipation, a "first fruits" of the new creation, and the sign of the final gathering together of all things into God. It was called to follow its Lord in living the kingdom in this present age, and thus to be a bridgehead of the advancing realm of God. In Acts, we see Luke's portrayal of this kingdom community in the making, a community of grace. From the outset, all are accepted equally into this fellowship—irrespective of where they come from, or what they bring. Through the conflict over the admission of Gentiles, grace continues to force its way out to the last and the least. In Acts 2:42-47, 4:32-35, and 5:12-18, the koinonia (Acts 2:42) brings together all members in brotherly and sisterly sharing, prayer and table fellowship, shared suffering and common ownership of property. The believers "devoted themselves to fellowship" (Acts 2:42), "held everything in common" (Acts 2:44) and "not one of them considered anything his private property" (Acts 4:32). "There was not a needy person among them, for those who owned land or houses sold them and brought the proceeds of the sale and laid it at the apostles' feet; it was then distributed according to every individual's need" (Acts 4:34,35). It is not clear whether the first Christians resigned all the personal possessions to a common fund, or whether they retained personal use until it was needed to relieve the poverty of others.

The New Testament church sought to live out its life under the guidance of the Spirit in continuing the kingdom attitude towards material possessions. The service of God and the sharing of life in the fellowship took priority. Their security was in God's provision through his people and all property was at the disposal of the community. Social distinctions were abolished and poverty was overcome.

Paul's letters prescribe a way of life for a community living by grace. Though there is less explicit reference to the poor or to the sharing of this world's goods in Paul's writing, 1 Cor. 11 implies the emergence of status divisions and a consequent failure to share in the Lord's Supper. Paul calls for a society in which each looks to the good of the other, in which there is "distribution to the need of all," hospitality; and the weakest, the least, and the most deprived are given the greatest honor (1 Cor. 12).

The collection for Jerusalem (2 Cor. 8, and Gal. 2:10) had the special theological significance of a thank offering on the part of Gentile churches to the Jerusalem church. It was a reversal of the usual practice, as those who had received the good news of God's grace responded by sharing with the poorer church from which the mission had come. Paul took the opportunity to expound his own understanding of giving as the implementation of justice, "It is only fair that you should help those who are in need. Then, when you are in need and they have plenty, they will help you. In this way, both are treated equally" (2 Cor. 8:14). The source of our giving is the grace of Christ, to which our own generosity in sharing must be a response. "You know the grace of our Lord Jesus Christ; rich as he was, he made himself poor for your sake, in order to make you rich by means of his poverty" (2 Cor. 8:9). As we in turn continue the mutual interchange in a fellowship of joy and sorrow, gifts and needs, we realize the unity in Christ of a church founded on love.

The church, for Paul, is itself the living expression of a grace which chooses and uses what is weak, poor, and despised in this world (1 Cor. 1: 18-30). In this church, the members are to mediate the gifts of Christ in mutual interdependence (1 Cor. 12; Rom. 12), in self-humiliation and self-giving (Phil. 2:5-8; 2 Cor. 8:9), and to live in anticipation of the kingdom of God. This involves the establishment of divine justice in love already correcting the distortions caused by men's sins (Romans 13:8-10; 1 Thess. 4:11,12; 2 Thess. 3:7-12). Whenever this pattern of community appeared to be breaking down, New Testament writers comment strongly. In James, there is an attack on the rich, and a pleading for the cause of the poor (James 1:9-11; 2:2-4; 5:1-6). 1 John 3:16-18 points to a failure in sharing as the one concrete example in the epistle about love in action.

Overall, the New Testament presents an impressive picture of the church as the model of God's purpose for humankind. As this purpose was embodied and expressed in the life of Jesus Christ, so his followers, in the Body of Christ, continue to carry the Gospel to the world. This Gospel is proclaimed by word and deed, and the shared life of the church is the visual aid that illustrates and conveys the grace of Christ. Changed attitudes and relationships among Christians carry through into a fundamental sharing of life at all levels. This community of grace proclaims vividly the new order of the kingdom, transforming the lives of individuals and challenging the whole social order.

The Good News to the Poor

The proclamation of the "good news of the kingdom" and its embodiment in Jesus and in the community that fully shares his life comes as a judgment on the ingrained, distorted social patterns of this world. Its values are turned upside down and its structures are questioned. A new order, a new pattern is here, into which all are invited. All who hear, turn, and come in are accepted through the grace which opens up to all people this new life shared with God.

It is hard for the poor to accept this entirely unexpected invitation because of their previous exclusion from the good things of life and their relegation in the old order to the sidelines and margins. But now they find themselves accepted and invited in first of all (Luke 4:18-19). The invitation is addressed specifically to them, "Come to me, all of you who are tired from carrying heavy loads" (Matt. 11:28). At last, the poor are able to see themselves as God created them, in their true dignity and worth. Now they are persons with something to contribute, something to share.

Just as they are inwardly healed and changed, so they are enabled to see the world through new eyes. They are no longer servants to the false structures that once threatened and trapped them. They see the central weaknesses, and know that the old patterns are already defeated and passing. In the new life of faith and the shared love of the believing community, they have fresh hope.

The rich also are summoned to discover themselves in God's sight and to recognize that they, too, are sinners in need of grace. For them it is much harder. They have so much they must lose (Matt. 19:16-21). It is hard for them to receive and respond to this invitation to live by grace, when security lies in wealth, power, and status. It is even harder to repent and, like Zacchaeus, to acknowledge that their wealth comes from a defrauding of the poor. Yet the same movement of grace can release the rich from their isolation and estrangement.

Both those who were poor and those who were rich, on entering into the death and risen life of Jesus Christ, find their place together in his kingdom community. Here those who know themselves accepted in him, can accept each other. Here the Magnificat is made visible. The mighty are put down from their seats, the poor lifted up and the hungry fed.

But those who cling to their wealth must, like the rich young ruler, be sent away empty.

The Evangelical Failure Among the Poor

Despite the universal and growing presence of urban poor people in the world and the biblical mandate compelling concern for the poor, there is often a great gulf between the church and the poor.

There is, however, increasing evidence of church leadership in Latin America dissociating itself from that identification with oppressive regimes and taking up the cause of the poor. Such courageous identification with urban poor by Archbishop Romero in San Salvador led to his assassination.

Most evangelistic efforts among the urban poor have borne little fruit.

Culture and class—The Christian church is seen to be trapped in a middle-class, establishment culture. There is an image of the church as aligned with the rich and powerful, which is confirmed by the social mobility drift of Christians from the urban poor to the middle-class areas and attitudes. This is often enhanced by incoming external evangelistic efforts exuding success and respectability, the imposition of the committee approach with its agendas, minutes, and accounts, and the control by professionals of church life.

The life of the church so often blocks the gospel. One national group said, "Within ourselves we discover an unwillingness to accept fully the pattern of the Incarnation. Even when we set out to work with the urban poor, we find that our institutions and organizations actually shield us from the painful realities of poverty and divide us from those who are poor." The long-established gulf between the church and the urban poor has often removed spiritual expectancy, and a fatalistic resignation has immobilized effort and prayer.

Wrong methods—Mission programs tend to work for, rather than work with, the urban poor. This lack of identification and attitude of superiority has led to a paternalism, which is quickly identified, resented, and rejected.

Where Are the Signs of Hope?

These include:

1. Social action groups—often centered on issues like race, housing, poverty, or justice.
2. Support and sharing groups operating on a "care and share" basis, and drawing individuals into group life.
3. Development groups with a holistic emphasis.
4. Renewal programs establishing locally controlled, often co-operative, services to maintain economic independence.
5. Cell-groups coming together to develop a deeper, indigenous, urban spirituality.
6. The spreading of the simple life-style movement.
7. New and imaginative forms of training for both professional and lay members of the church.
8. The entry of Christians into the worlds of labor, politics, and economics.

Current experience: It is clear from evidence and experience that mission work has already begun with the building up of small communities, teams, or cells. In Brazil alone, there are more than 80,000 "base communities" with over 2,000,000 people, largely rooted in Catholicism. Evangelical experience came from Hong Kong where— through such communities—600 people within 10 years have been drawn to Christ from among the poorest workers. In the inner cities of Britain, small, newly planted churches are growing up to cover people of many cultures and ethnic origins. Established churches entered renewal through the new life springing from "base communities" emerging in many denominations and areas.

Social rightness: These communities convey the possibility of caring, healing, integration, and purpose to those who have known harshness, hurt, division, and hopelessness. Where economic pressures have affected the capacity to make choices or decisions, an accepting, or affirming group will encourage the development of gifts and the confidence required to face responsibility. This can only take place within a nurturing environment. In such a caring community, the way of Christ as a lived and living reality will become a genuine option for the poor. Although the groups vary in form and style according to the context, source, and leadership, it will become a redemptive presence with indigenous leadership rooted in society, demonstrating God's love, and encouraging participation in God's kingdom.

Solidarity in standing alongside others in the struggle for justice, equality, and opportunity, over against wrongful imprisonment, racism, and exploitation.

Awareness-raising in the understanding of the needs of a neighborhood and the reasons for its plight, in the gathering of resources to bring change, in the training of basic skill in community development, and in the unlocking of individual skills and confidence.

Biblical pattern: In "base communities" the "word is made flesh." Faith, hope, and love are experienced in action. The groups embody and express the gospel. Within them, is found koinonia-fellowship, body-ministry, and personal dignity and destiny. Through them, the Good News is announced openly, visually, and internationally. Within them, relevant Bible study and corporate prayer tie in with the everyday realities of life. Through them, joyful participation in worship, new styles of living within simplicity and stewardship and directness in evangelism confront neighbors and friends.

Through the flexibility and diversity of base communities, Christian presence emerges to confront individuals within urban society at many levels.

Residential Involvement as Christians choose to live as one of the poor, sharing their lives and neighborhoods, living in interdependence with them.

Residential Communities as households, networks, and varying communities learn to share lives, possessions, and commitment to each other and the neighborhood.

Service to others as Christians share in the struggle for homes, food, medical treatment, employment, legal advice, counseling, literacy; operate necessary amenities such as launderettes, eating houses, crisis centers.

Micro-loans: A success story

One of the most successful tools missional NGO's have used in recent years is what is called micro-loans, or micro credit.

The Bible clearly sees charging interest on loans, particularly on loans to the poor, as wrong and Jewish bankers in NT times **paid** interest (Matthew 25:27, Luke 19:23) but did not charge it. They used money deposited with them to trade with and the profits from the trade paid the interest to the depositor. From a Christian perspective it is not wrong to receive interest on money invested or deposited but it is wrong to charge interest, especially to the poor. There are nine clear injunctions on this in Scripture and because they are so little preached on and yet of so great a consequence for world trade I am reproducing them in full here.

(Exodus 22:25 NASB) "If you lend money to My people, to the poor among you, you are not to act as a creditor to him; you shall not charge him interest.

(Leviticus 25:36-37 NKJV) 'Take no usury or interest from him; but fear your God, that your brother may live with you. {37} 'You shall not lend him your money for usury, nor lend him your food at a profit.

(Deuteronomy 23:19-20 NASB) "You shall not charge interest to your countrymen: interest on money, food, or anything that may be loaned at interest. {20} "You may charge interest to a foreigner, but to your countryman you shall not charge interest, so that the LORD your God may bless you in all that you undertake in the land which you are about to enter to possess.

(Psalms 15:5 NASB) He does not put out his money at interest, nor does he take a bribe against the innocent. He who does these things will never be shaken.

117

(Proverbs 28:8 NASB) He who increases his wealth by interest and usury, Gathers it for him who is gracious to the poor.

(Ezekiel 18:5-9 NKJV) But if a man is just And does what is lawful and right; ....{8} If he has not exacted usury Nor taken any increase, But has withdrawn his hand from iniquity And executed true judgment between man and man; {9} If he has walked in My statutes And kept My judgments faithfully; He is just; He shall surely live!" Says the Lord GOD.

(Ezekiel 18:12-13 NKJV) If he has oppressed the poor and needy, Robbed by violence, Not restored the pledge, Lifted his eyes to the idols, Or committed abomination; {13} If he has exacted usury Or taken increase; Shall he then live? He shall not live! If he has done any of these abominations, He shall surely die; His blood shall be upon him.

(Ezekiel 18:17 NASB) he keeps his hand from the poor, does not take interest or increase, but executes My ordinances, and walks in My statutes; he will not die for his father's iniquity, he will surely live.

(Ezekiel 22:6-13 NKJV) "Look, the princes of Israel: each one has used his power to shed blood in you. {7} ...{12} "In you they take bribes to shed blood; you take usury and increase; you have made profit from your neighbors by extortion, and have forgotten Me," says the Lord GOD. {13} "Behold, therefore, I beat My fists at the dishonest profit which you have made, and at the bloodshed which has been in your midst.

You cannot get clearer than that! God regards charging interest, especially to the poor as wicked and dishonest profiteering. This is well illustrated during the time of Nehemiah:

> (Nehemiah 5:1-13 NKJV)   And there was a great outcry of the people and their wives against their Jewish brethren. {2} For there were those who said, "We, our sons, and our daughters are many; therefore let us get grain, that we may eat and live." {3} There were also some who said, "We have mortgaged our lands and vineyards and houses, that we might buy grain because of the famine." {4} There were also those who said, "We have borrowed money for the king's tax on our lands and vineyards. {5} "Yet now our flesh is as the flesh of our brethren, our children as their children; and indeed we are forcing our sons and our daughters to be slaves, and some of our daughters have been brought into slavery. It is not in our power to redeem them, for other men have our lands and vineyards." {6} And I became very angry when I heard their outcry and these words. {7} After serious thought, I rebuked the nobles and rulers, and said to them, "Each of you is exacting usury from his brother." So I called a great assembly against them. {8} And I said to them, "According to our ability we have redeemed our Jewish brethren who were sold to the nations. Now indeed, will you even sell your brethren? Or should they be sold to us?" Then they were silenced and found nothing to say. {9} Then I said, "What you are doing is not good. Should you not walk in the fear of our God because of the reproach of the nations, our enemies?" {10} "I also, with my brethren and my servants, am lending them

money and grain. Please, let us stop this usury! {11} "Restore now to them, even this day, their lands, their vineyards, their olive groves, and their houses, also a hundredth of the money and the grain, the new wine and the oil, that you have charged them." {12} So they said, "We will restore it, and will require nothing from them; we will do as you say." Then I called the priests, and required an oath from them that they would do according to this promise. {13} Then I shook out the fold of my garment and said, "So may God shake out each man from his house, and from his property, who does not perform this promise. Even thus may he be shaken out and emptied." And all the assembly said, "Amen!" and praised the LORD. Then the people did according to this promise.

Here the interest charge by the rich was forcing people into slavery and destitution and to the loss of houses and lands. They were foreclosing on their brethren! Nehemiah's response was fierce and unequivocal and sealed with a curse that the house of those who did not comply with the order to restore all that was taken would be shaken out and emptied by God. Also Nehemiah and all who followed him graciously and freely lent food and money to the poor.

If you have ever struggled to pay off a car, a credit card or a mortgage you will know how devastating interest can be. Frequently you end up paying double the original cost of the goods by the time the interest period is over. Biblically speaking, the only justifiable interest is a small charge to match the inflation rate as that preserves the real value of the money lent. Above that the lender is starting to exploit the poverty and desperation of the lender.

Charging interest deepens poverty and robs people of their power to make wealth. Unfortunately I have seen microfinance schemes designed to 'help the poor' that charge as much as 2 to 3 per cent per month - that is up to 40% plus per annum. Even Christian microfinance schemes are run on the most impractical idea that the poor will borrow the money, start a small business and then repay the capital in one year plus interest rates of 2-3% per month (equivalent to 25%-40% annual interest rates). This requires the small business, in its first year of operation, to make 140% on capital invested - before the owner receives a single dollar in profit or wages from the enterprise. To ask this of the poor starting out in business is grossly unfair.

Lending to the poor can increase their power to make wealth if it is used to purchase a means of production of some sort. But the power to make wealth is in turn decreased by interest payments. The interest payments ensure that funds generated from the means of production simply return to the lender. At the end of 12 months the microfinance scheme has received their capital plus 40% back again but what has the poor person got "in hand" after a years work? Probably nothing, other than the means of production (such as a sewing machine), that they purchased. They are unlikely to have made a wage at all. The interest payments have entirely consumed their power to make wealth.

Some may ask "If the micro-finance schemes were stopped from charging interest to the poor how could the poor get access to capital?" In some senses that is a good question, in other ways it is a quite mistaken question. "Access to capital" implies that the poor are best off starting a small business, which needs capital.

Thus I believe that micro financers should rethink itself as an interest free overdraft facility for the poor.

If Christian micro-finance chooses to stay with starting small businesses I think they should not lend money to any enterprise, no matter how small or how well intentioned, that does not have a workable and thought-through business plan. To my mind there is a certain amount of glorious hopefulness among those who help the poor with financial schemes. Ideas that a bank manager or accountant would say are quite impractical and commercially non-viable are funded in the "hope" that they will work - and out of a genuine desire to be kind and gracious and to give people a chance. But what actually happens? The vast majority of such hopeful enterprises fail, leaving the person with a debt. The person is worse off than before. If the person cannot pay their debt and defaults on the loan the micro finance scheme loses capital and has to seek more funding. The "kindness' does not produce a winner, in fact it produces two losers. The hard reality of business life is that undercapitalized businesses frequently fail and micro finance is just that – micro. There is no spare capital and not much room for mistakes. Unless the venture is very well thought through from the start the likelihood of failure is high. Thus if micro finance is to succeed in increasing the wealth of the poor it must be interest free and it must insist on adequate level of capitalization and on sound business plans. For an interesting read try Gina Neff's article "MicroThis, MicroThat Left Business Observer #74, October 1996 – just one quote: "For example, Grameen rules insist that its borrowers own their homes - not unlike the assumption that shoeless women have bootstraps. Evidently Bangladeshi homeless women don't count as the poorest of the poor. And unfortunately, Grameen borrowers are staying poor. After 8 years of borrowing, 55% of Grameen households still aren't able to meet their basic nutritional needs - so many women are using their loans to buy food rather than invest in business."

Even worse are the pawnbrokers that charge what is known as "5 – 6". That is for every 5 dollars loaned you pay back 6 dollars, generally three to six months later. That amounts to 4 per cent per month or over 50% per annum. Since the poor have regular financial crises when it comes to medical bills or school fees; they have little choice but to borrow money at outrageous interest rates. The alternative is to watch their family members die or their children drop out of school. Thus loans are a necessary part of survival. The pawnbrokers and other lenders are thus preying on the very vulnerability of the poor. When the poor pay 40%-50% annual interest on borrowed money their power to make wealth is not being increased but rather is being halved. Pawnbrokers also are "secured" creditors able to sell what has been deposited as collateral on the loan. They also lend money for any purpose, not just starting a small business. Thus the funds are simply used on household expenditure, the interest rates consume any power to make wealth and in the event of a default their goods are sold.

Interest has national and international implications as well. This has become known as the "International Debt Crisis" and is being addressed by a group known as the Jubilee 2000 coalition, which seeks relief from debt for a range of poor countries and especially a group known as the Heavily Indebted Poor Countries such as Mozambique. In such countries the interest repayments alone outstrip GDP by a factor of three or four times. Because the obligation to pay back these loans is primary and onerous the money cannot be used for public infrastructure such as health or even for food. Some calculations estimate that 7 million children die each year simply as a result of the debt crisis. The six million who died during the Jewish Holocaust are remembered because the Nazis killed them. The 7 million who die each and every year from the greed of the world banking system, however are simply forgotten.

If poverty is to be solved interest in all its forms must be abolished as the Muslims have done and as Scriptures prescribe; or at least reduced to the level of the annual CPI increase. Can this be done? There is increasing attention being paid to "non-interest income" in the banking sector as interest rates are at their lowest levels for many years. Canadian Banking Commission shows that 51% of bank income came from non-interest sources.

Note that 51% of bank revenue is obtained WITHOUT CHARGING INTEREST.

Could 100% of bank revenue be obtained without charging interest to the poor? Looking at the 49% that is designated as "Interest Income" we find it is broken down into mortgages, personal loans, commercial loans and banks own investments. Commercial loans are in the millions of dollar category and generally do not affect the poor. The banks own investments are in the tens of billions of dollars and are outside this category as well. That leaves mortgages and personal loans as being of concern. Exact figures for each of these segments are not given in the report so I have to take an "educated guess" that mortgages and personal loans would constitute say one-third of the 49% that would be about 16 to 17 per cent of the total bank revenue. Of these mortgages and personal loans the poorest 30% of the country would perhaps account for 5% of the mortgages and personal loans (by loan volume). Five percent of 17% is about 0.85%. If 0.85% of the revenue comes from charging interest to the poor - then 99.15% % does not come from charging interest to the poor. So we can see that banks in Canada now earn around 99% of their current revenue without charging interest to the poor. Even if my figures are a factor of five out that would still mean that banks would earn 95% of their revenue without charging interest to the poor. It does not seem impossible that they could make this 100%.

Obviously a much deeper analysis with the exact figures is necessary but this small example helps puncture the myth that banks would "go broke" if they did not charge interest to the poor. Banking is perfectly feasible without charging interest on loans to those in need. There are many other profitable sectors of financial activity for banks to engage in. Muslim banks that are strict about their adherence to *sharia* law go into partnership with the person much as a venture capitalist does in the West. A July 5th 2001 New York Times article discusses the emerging market for Muslim banking in the USA with its dual requirements of a) no interest b) the lender and borrower share risk equally (thus the bank cannot foreclose in most cases). Large banks such as HSBC and finance companies like Freddie Mac are trying to tailor products, mainly house and car loans, for the USA's 7 million Muslims. Up until now this kind of lending has mainly been the province of small co-operatives. The nature of the lending varies but seems to be mainly based on a partnership contract between the lender and the home-buyer. One institution is funding the lending by making a bond issue on the loans and promoting it overseas to wealthy and religiously correct Muslims.

Outside of the USA, in the developing world interest is crushing them. Interest is a huge problem for three reasons. Firstly government borrowings have the nation heavily indebted, secondly the peso is falling and it is harder to pay those obligations, thirdly the average person pays anywhere between 18% to 50% annual interest on personal borrowings. Repayment periods are short, and deposits are high, typically a car is purchased on 50% deposit - "half down, the rest in two years".

The ability to earn decent interest on savings and investments is almost nil for the average person. Most are receiving only 1 or 2% return in real (after inflation) terms on their deposits in the banks. Many receive a negative real return. Banks routinely collapse taking depositors savings with them.

The repayment rate for most micro finance schemes is the reverse of the Grameen bank in Bangladesh where 95% do not default. Here 95% do not repay their funds and the micro-finance loan is seen as a handout. The vast majority of micro finance schemes fold and the only successful Christian micro finance scheme charges 3% per month interest (40% per year) and is highly commercially driven. Over 90% of co-operatives collapse due to corruption.

Serve the Homeless

Currently an estimated 125 million people live outside the countries of their birth. According to 1995 official UN figures, 13.2 million people of that total are refugees.

That is only the official tip of the iceberg. The statistics do not include those who have sought unofficial asylum in other countries or have been displaced within their own national borders (UNFPA 1997:14-15). Accurate head counts are hard to take as Bosnians and Kurds take to the world's roads.

Some are driven by environmental problems-the loss of farmland, forests, and pasture. Others move in search of a better life for themselves and their families. Political conflict fuels migration within countries as well as across borders.

Africa may represent the bleakest picture. As a continent it has become itself a "huge refugee camp" (Myth and Cahill 1993:15). Displacement created by ethnic and political conflicts, by drought and disaster, finds Eritreans in Sudan, Angolans in Zaire, Liberians and Chadians in Nigeria, Hutu and Tutsi struggling in Rwanda. In Mozambique a seventeen-year civil war (1975-1992) has displaced more than four million within the country. And nearly two million more have fled across their border to Malawi, South Africa, Tanzania, and Zimbabwe.

Across the globe the same pattern of displacement and migration shift repeats itself-

Afghanis to Pakistan, Khmers to Thailand and Malaysia, Albanians to Italy. During the Nicaraguan repression under Somoza, 100,000 were sent into exile in 1978. "Since the end of the Vietnam war in 1975, over two million people have fled from Vietnam, Laos, and Cambodia" (Mieth and Cahill 1993:9). Since 1991 some 40,000 Haitians have attempted passage to the United States. Refugees are on the move by the millions.

Migration and Urbanization

"Where do all the uprooted go, with or without their families? Millions head for the big town, adding to the chaos of the ever-expanding suburbs, creating more and more 'favellas'" (Jacques 1986:44). Migration patterns, whether internal or international, are often toward the cities. By the year 2005, estimates the United Nations, urban areas are expected to be home to more than half of the world's people. And migration will be a significant reason for that growth.

Bearing the major brunt of today's refugee problem are the Third World countries and cities. "Today's refugee populations are most heavily in the world of poor nations" (Cogswell 1983:27-28). Tightly controlled quota systems in the West process entrances individual by individual; in developing countries they come in waves. Squatter settlements spring up and cling to the hillsides of Rio de Janeiro and Lima. The tombs of Cairo's City of the Dead become homes for thousands of dispossessed. A World Vision report estimates "the number of urban squatters across the Philippines reached 18 million in 1992" (Power 1996:19). And forming the largest part of this refugee population are women and children (UNFPA 1997:15).

Living on land they do not own, thousands of refugee households are displaced every year by demolitions and eviction notices. Where they exist, federal and city development programs, already stretched by limited budgets, are swamped by the needs of the new arrivals-jobs, housing, health, basic human services. Poverty becomes the dominant social problem for the host city.

Global Fatigue

Against these pressures, compassion in the developing countries becomes jaded by economic realities. One day's solution becomes the next day's problem. Where does one begin in a place like Calcutta, India? It "has survived two successive waves of three million refugees each. The result is a city of 16 million-equal to the entire urban population of Australia-in which there are 500,000 people who live their entire lives on the street" (Linthicum 1994:2).

There are signs that western compassion is also drying up in the face of these massive needs. Europe's countries are repeating a slogan heard often after World War II: "the boat is full." The number of refugees admitted to the United States has declined since 1992 by forty percent (Gedda 1997:A4). Even our western vocabulary is beginning to sound to some like a negative echo. The United States talks about "wetbacks," "boat people," "illegals," "the Palestinian problem." Canada speaks about the "plane people," the principal port of refugee entry for her being the airport.

Biblical Reminders

The people of God have tasted the plight of refugees before. Abraham's flight to Egypt from drought (Gen. 12:10) and his life-long dwelling in tents was copied in the life of Isaac (Gen. 26:1-6) and in Joseph's sojourn in Egypt as a slave. Four hundred years in Egypt marked Israel as "strangers in a country not their own.... enslaved and mistreated" (Acts 7:6).

And against this experience of rejection and exploitation, God made their own treatment of strangers and exiles a criterion of fidelity to God's covenant: "Do not mistreat an alien or oppress him, for you were aliens in Egypt" (Ex. 22:21; 23:9; Lev. 19:33-34; Zech. 7:10). God's curse awaited his own children who "withheld justice from the alien, the fatherless or the widow" (Deut. 27:19), his blessing for those who shared (Deut. 24:19-20; 26:12-13).

Jesus was the stranger par excellence. He was the refugee child who went to Egypt in flight (Matt. 2:13-22) and returned as the last Moses for his exodus departure at Calvary (Luke 9:31). To the broken and abused he was the promised good news of jubilee redemption (Luke 4:18-19); to the leftovers of society-prostitutes, the poor, and publicans-he brought invitations to the heavenly banquet of God (Luke 5:30-31; 15:1-2).

Now his disciples, like him "aliens and strangers in the world" (I Pet. 2:11). follow him in ministry. As refugees they wander "among the nations" (Luke 24:47), carrying the good news of his salvation and healing (Matt. 28:18-20). They are to reach out in compassion to the stranger (Matt. 25:36, 40). And in caring for strangers they care for Jesus. Like "good Samaritans" (a contradiction in terms for any first century Israelite), they are to define neighbor as "anyone in need" (Luke 10:36-38).

Today's Christian Challenge

Across the boundaries of today's world that Samaritan call still rings. Organizations like Habitat for Humanity, the TEAR fund, World Relief and World Vision are speaking in compassion by word and deed to wide global needs.

And closer to the grassroots level, Christians are networking together with their neighbors to combine Bible study and community action. Wells are dug in African slums neglected by the city. In Russia the International Church of St. Petersburg sends teams to the city's four main metro stops, looking for the homeless "children at risk." Tijuana's Unidad Cristiana Church, started in 1982 with four people, has grown now to over 4,000 members. It uses its seventy-three home Bible study centers to reach out to community needs through a ministry called "Mercy." When heavy rains left a large number of people without shelter or food, the church provided food, clothing and materials for housing construction. Church members contributed voluntary labor. Says its pastor, Fermin Garcia, "We want to teach people to give and not receive . . . . The church should be where the need is the greatest" (Valencia 1994:26).

What makes the church different from any other social agency offering cups of cold water to refugees? We offer them in the name of Jesus. What does the church give to the struggle between Croats and Serbs that cannot be duplicated elsewhere? Reconciliation in Christ as the beginning of healing. Where can the church appeal in the conflict between the powerful and the powerless? To the justice and compassion of the Father.

Ann Judson, wife of the famous pioneer to Burma, saw the "bridges of God" among the Siamese displaced there. She studied Siamese for eighteen months and translated a catechism and Matthew's Gospel for their use. Melinda Rankin, a school teacher, saw those same "bridges." She became burdened over the Mexican braceros and their families who worked the summer-harvests near Brownsville, Texas, and then returned to their homes across the border. In 1852 she started a school for the workers' children. After the reform of Juarez she moved across the border and worked in Monterrey. Ten years later she returned in broken health to her home. She left behind fourteen congregations and the beginning of the Presbyterian Church in Mexico.

Incarnational Lives

Case Study: Father Beltran

Father Benigno Beltran worked with garbage scavengers in Manila, the capital of the Philippines, helping to transform them into a productive Christian community. His ministry has earned many honors, including World Vision's 1997 Robert W. Pierce Award for Christian Service. But Fr. Ben points to obedience: "I would not do otherwise. Jesus would not do otherwise."

When Father Ben Beltran came to Smokey Mountain 20 years ago, he saw a garbage heap almost 100 feet high, reeking of methane gas and polluting the air and water. The dumpsite - ironically named for its resemblance to the Smokey Mountains in the United States - was a blight on the landscape, a political hot potato, a shameful symbol of urban decay. It was also home to a large squatter population.

The young Catholic priest resolved, "In a Christian country, there should not be 25,000 people surviving by picking through the garbage." That day, he began to dream of a new Smokey Mountain.

Now, the dream is being realized by Sambayanang Kristiyano, Smokey Mountain's self-sufficient, spiritually-strong community. Under Fr. Ben's tutelage, community members have turned from humiliating scavenging to better jobs, and converted the squatter settlement into something resembling a real neighborhood. The success earned Fr. Ben international attention, funding, and access to Philippine President Fidel Ramos. But to this modest man, none of that equals his long, loving association with Smokey Mountain, where children take his hand and press it to their foreheads in a gesture of honor.

Going to the Mountain

Fr. Ben's life is inextricably entwined with Smokey Mountain. He has become more a product of this place than the forests of Mindinao (a southern Philippine island) where he was born in 1946. His parents, Benigno Sr., a retired government official, and Concepcion, a teacher, recall that Ben, the oldest of five, was drawn to the religious life early, signing up to be a church altar boy before he could see over the altar. A serious student, he was valedictorian of both his elementary and high school graduating classes.

After college, Ben entered the seminary of the Society of the Divine Word, assisted by Benigno Sr., who quit smoking and drinking and put that money toward Ben's expenses. Although originally interested in missions work in Africa, the newly-ordained Fr. Ben seemed destined to teach in the seminary. But he was troubled by his inability to connect theory with practice. His solution: "I decided to look for the poorest of the poor and just be with them." He asked the Sisters of Charity, Mother Theresa's order, to help him find a needy place. They sent him to Smokey Mountain.

Since 1954, Manila's government had been dumping garbage on this former fishing area. As the dump grew, so did the number of scavengers - people broken

135

by the hardships of the city who had no choice but to live among refuse and rats. Politicians, journalists, and aid workers came to gawk at the dumpsite, quickly fleeing the stench and crushing poverty. Fr. Ben stayed.

"I was not trained for breathing in smoke and particles 24 hours a day, or eating inside mosquito nets because otherwise the food would be full of flies," he says. "Nobody can train you for that." He developed chronic bronchitis and allergies.

Fr. Ben led the celebration of the Eucharist every Sunday in a run-down chapel that was later repaired to become the Church of the Risen Christ. "[The Mass] was the answer to the people's prayers," Fr. Ben says. "It gave them a sense of identity." He walked around the shantytown and talked to people, gradually earning their trust.

Fr. Ben's vision for the community crystallized in 1983. The government, eyeing the financial opportunities of a revitalized waterfront, forcibly resettled the Smokey Mountain squatters to another area. "The people came back because there were no jobs," Fr. Ben recalls. "They were starving to death." He set up a tarpaulin for a temporary chapel, and the work began in earnest. Starting with the natural leaders, he began training people to form "basic Christian communities" - families grouped into cells with elected leaders representing their interests on various problem-solving committees, including livelihood, health, education, culture, spirituality, sport, and housing.

Some community factions opposed the work. Fr. Ben received death threats. Once, a grenade was hurled onto the roof of his living quarters. It didn't explode, nor did it deter him. He dismisses the incident as a nuisance "on equal terms with the flies." His parents remember Ben's perseverance: "I cannot run away from problems," he told them.

Smokey Mountain changed Fr. Ben. "I learned that God is speaking through the poor," he says. "We should not think that only theologians understand the Bible. We have not listened to the poor. Just because they are unlettered does not mean that the truths of the Bible cannot be revealed to them."

Fr. Ben implemented Bible sharing, in which community members read and discuss Scripture, empowering them to take a more active role in their faith without cues from clergy - a break with tradition in this predominantly Catholic country. "Even in our absence, people can talk about problems and settle issues," says Fr. Jerome Marquez, who joined the Smokey Mountain staff in 1995. "It makes the Bible the key to community organizing, sustenance, and growth."

As funding came in from the Philippine and U.S. governments, private donors, and relief agencies (World Vision supported leadership training), the community launched education programs and built a water system, a multi-purpose center, and paved walkways between people's homes and the dump. Such changes had great impact on residents such as Christine Calisterio, who used to be shunned at the market because she smelled after trudging through muddy garbage. Families also moved from their squatter shacks into temporary housing, and soon will live in attractive permanent apartments. "I only started to believe in miracles when I came here," says Fr. Jerome.

Missionaries to the Asphalt Jungle

The Society of the Divine Word seminary in Tagaytay, a three-hour drive from Manila, offers a glimpse into the other side of Fr. Ben's life - contemplation regeneration. The quiet seminary, surrounded by lush banana and coffee plants and colorful bougainvillea, provides the perfect setting.

Fr. Ben teaches here two days a week, preparing young seminarians for urban ministry. "You have to read and keep up with theorists, otherwise you run out of ideas," he explains.

Part of Fr. Ben's effectiveness in the classroom is that he lives what he teaches, says Fr. Jerome, a former student. "[The work] becomes very concrete when you see it in action."

"A new humanity is being born in the city, and that's why missionaries should go there," insists Fr. Ben. "Our romanticism tells us we should go to places like New Guinea. But the decisions influencing the lives of hundreds of millions are not made in the villages, but in the asphalt jungle."

Recently he presented a multi-media symposium on "The Church in the City," introducing seminarians to global urbanization trends and the complex needs of the urban poor, ending with a challenge to the church to respond. The information overwhelmed many of the young men from rural regions. But in the open forum, one student commented, "Hope for the city is in our hands. We are the church. But before we can change the world, we must change ourselves."

Such is the task of those who will follow in Fr. Ben's footsteps. At 51, he is ready to leave Smokey Mountain in the capable hands of community leaders. At the year's end he will travel to the United States to set up an urban ministry training program with missiologist Ray Bakke. There are, after all, many Smokey Mountains in the world needing the "new heavens and new earth" promises of Isaiah 65.

"What we have reaped here is all because a man had a vision," says Fr. Jerome. "It's like Jesus' vision for everybody - the kingdom of God."

Professor Harvey Conn

Harvey Conn, professor at Westminster Seminary tells a story:

"Some months ago I was visiting the Midwest, and a friend invited me to go to a midnight prayer meeting. We went into this row house and up a set of rickety stairs and opened the door. There was this long table and about twelve people sitting around it, all with Bibles in front of them with beer cans strewn all over the smoke-filled room.

The Bible study leader was at the end, smoking this long, black cigar - and she really enjoyed it. At the other end of the table was this guy, built like Sylvester Stallone, wearing a black T-shirt with a white skull on it. On one arm was a big tattoo, a heart with the word *mother* on it and a big dagger through it.

So we sat down for a two-hour Bible study. Having been teaching at a typical white suburban theological seminary where everything's safe, I had my doubts when things started, but when we were done, I had no doubts about what was going on. These were people who really loved the Lord, most of them brand new believers. The gentleman at the end of the table with the tattoo had been responsible for leading almost everyone there to Christ.

These were bikers. They wouldn't feel much at home in our community or in most of our churches. Two or three of the members of the Bible study were former members of Hell's Angels. A member of the Christian Biker's Association, the fellow who started the Bible study spends six months of the year with his wife on the road, and his whole ministry is spent trying to reach bikers for Jesus. "Most outsiders," he told me, "are turned off by the beer and cigars. You ought to have seen what they were smoking and drinking a few months ago. Some Christians start at 1; other, at -3." I had found another unreached people group, one I didn't have to travel overseas to find. "

In New York City his seminary class surveyed a six-block area to find out who was serving the people of the area. It was not the churches.

The seminary class found only three Christian groups and churches, and only one of those was working with the people in that area. The bars in the area were much more aware of people groups than the church, There were gay bars, singles bars, bars for the theater crowd and bars for newspaper people. Remember the opening line of the *Cheers* theme song, " . . . where everybody knows your name"?

The early Christian church looked a lot like one of these special clubs, I suspect. That's how they survived at first in the city. They had their regular meetings, they had their initiation rites, they looked a little kooky, they had their special meals, but they were a different kind of club. They were the only club that existed for the sake of its non-members. Always before our eyes, says Paul in his letters, must be those on the outside.

Artisans, says Paul, are to lead a quiet life, to mind their own business and to work with their hands (I Thess 4:11). Why? That their "daily life may win the respect of outsiders" (I Thess 4:12). Likewise, the Corinthian Christians must put no stumbling block before Jews and Greeks. The exercise of the gift of tongues in public assembly is to be restrained if visiting unbelievers get the wrong idea and think we Christians are insane. Any practices judged as disgraceful by the Gentiles must be curtailed (I Cor 11:4-6). Colossians 4:5 sums it up: "Behave wisely toward the outsiders, and cash in your opportunities."

Evelyn Quema, a short, stout, single Filipina, is barely noticeable in a crowd of women her age. At the age of 22 she gave up her desire to be a lawyer or a doctor and moved to the city of Baguio. She arrived on a Thursday with six dollars and no place to live. By Sunday she had conducted a church service for thirty and saw four conversions. Three years later she had planted four churches and started eleven outstations, one of them five hours away by bus. She had seen 300 solid conversions to Christ and several hundred more professions that she had not been able to follow up. Miriam Adeney, who tells this story, adds, "There are hundreds of Christian women like Evelyn in Southeast Asia."

Many of the poor I talk to say "I love Jesus. I just don't love his church. The picture is the same around the world. The church in too many cities listens to too many sermons on success rather than suffering while many feel left out in the ecclesiastical cold.

The industrial workers of Taiwan - three million of them - complain, "that the message of local churches is irrelevant to their daily life and most programs are geared toward the needs of the intellectuals or the middle class." Over 40% of Singapore's workforce is blue collar, production-industry workers. Yet only 4% of them are Christians.

At the bottom of society's value scale, and often the church's, are the poor, the squatters, and the new urban migrants. Forty-six percent of Mexico City's population, 67% of Calcutta's, 60% of Kinshasa's, live in slums. And the gap between them and the church now grows into a gulf.

A missionary recounted how he had targeted Japanese businessmen for Christ, inviting them to play golf with him. Their response to this "golf evangelism" was largely negative, but one of the caddies listened as they walked and talked. He in turn talked to other caddies, many of whom came to Christ through his witness. This missionary was wise enough to see what the Holy Spirit was doing and shifted his attention to a people group he had never seen before - Japanese golf caddies, the poor, and the invisible.

You watch for the footprints of the Lord in the sands of your ministry and you follow that trail.

Viv Grigg, a New Zealander, has made the same discovery about Jesus, "a companion to the poor." In 1979 he moved into Tatalon, a squatter community of 14,500 people, jammed into six city blocks in Manila. Now he pleads for the Lord's people to join him in creating Christian communities in the slums and shantytowns of the world. A new mission board has come out of his kingdom perspective called Servants Among the Poor. An old vision has been renewed: mobile men and women, freed for pioneering, prophetic, evangelistic church planting among the poor. "The greatest mission surge in history has entirely missed the greatest migration in history, the migration of Third World peasants to great mega-cities."

My Incarnational Lesson on Global Morality

Cities like Corinth or Colombo don't let you get away with dividing your Christian life into safety zones - one zone labeled faith, another the world. Ask Malcolm X? American racism turned him from talkative Christianity to what he saw as real brotherhood in Islam. Ask the Black Christians of Soweto. A plea for peace without justice can turn good news into cheap grace. "I was sick and you did not look after me; I was under the ban and you never visited me." Ask the Blacks and Latinos who come to Urbana. Ask them why you have to search so hard to find their brothers and sisters on the mission field abroad or on this platform at Urbana or on the mission boards represented at the armory. It's hard to hear "Go into all the world" when the same voices don't also say, "Come into all our neighborhoods."

Paul saw a social revolution brewing in the things we now identify as "church matters." A simple table meal to remember the Lord's death shatters social hierarchies long held sacred. At Corinth the wealthy apparently were making the Lord's Supper into a "private dinner party" (I Cor 11:21). And when the meal was over, the haves were drunk and the have-nots were hungry. Paul calls for a new kind of urban social order to be built from the table and the sacrifice that had prepared it (I Cor 10:16-17; 11:18-19). Wealth in the body of Christ becomes an opportunity to serve, prestige a call to humility.

None of this is easy in the city. Political and social networks fit together too tightly. You may find yourself one day a missionary pastor in a Central American country, the members of your congregation united in their commitment to Christ but divided in their political allegiances. Late one evening a knock may come to your door, there in front of you stands a member of your congregation, a brother in Christ with strong anti-government sympathies. There is a bullet in his arm; blood drips down his coat. "Pastor," he asks, "can I stay the night with you?" Suddenly your Christian response to a brother becomes a political decision.

More than ten years ago I was in an Iraqi village, an isolated village with no electricity. I was talking that night on the love of Christ and how Christians love one another, and at the end asked if there were any questions. An old man raised his hand. "I have a question, sir," he said. "If Christians are supposed to love one another, how do you explain what happened to Martin Luther King Jr.?"

There I was in a mountain canyon in the middle of nowhere and this old farmer with a goathair coat asked me about the racist murder of an American civil rights leader. Suddenly I discovered that the questions of racism and mission work are not two separate issues.

William Shepherd

In 1890 the Southern Presbyterian Church sent to the Congo a man who had learned these things. William Henry Shepherd spent twenty years in Africa. Respected by the Africans, he was called "Shoppit Monine, the Great Sheppard." Working among the Bokuba people, he showed a cultural respect and sensitivity for things African seldom seen among missionaries of his day. He knew how large this simple gospel was.

The Jesus that he preached was revolutionary in African society. For example, he resisted the custom of killing a slave to accompany a recently deceased master. He protested against the practice of trial by poison. When the Belgian government imposed a heavy food tax on the people, he protested. The tax forced the Africans to work for Europeans to pay it, a subtle form of colonialism. In addition, the government used soldiers who were cannibals to collect the tax. Shepherd discovered that the tax-collecting efforts were a cover for slave raids and for cannibalism. His protests brought the entire issue to the attention of King Leopold of Belgium. Strained relations with the government and with his mission finally brought him back to the States in retirement in 1910.

Sheppard had gone to Africa when the White Churches had almost no interest in Africa for Christ. Sheppard was Black, one of the 113 American Blacks who served in Africa from 1877 to 1900.

Who can tell how many Bakubans heard the word of Christ and believed because they saw Sheppard standing for the oppressed and the sinned against. It is an incarnational life like this that will yet stir the hearts of the urban world's poor.

Urban ministry is often focused on helping the urban poor. Distortions in this are common. Many ministries are so intent on poverty alleviation that evangelistic zeal is lost, others mistake "holistic" for comprehensive and fragment themselves by trying to run too many different kinds of programs, yet others become crass extensions of prosperity teaching while others see the poor as "in need of values" and descend into almost Victorian moralizing.

St Francis, The Wolf And The City

The legend of St. Francis and the Wolf at is a metaphor for the saintly Christian response to hunger and poverty.

The wolf can be any problem that presses the people into a fight or flight response. A problem, which the city consistently fails to solve, and which tears them apart day and night without mercy. Whatever is "tearing a community apart" – that is its Wolf.

The Wolf killed to satisfy its hunger, but it did so in a lawless and uncontrolled way bringing judgment on itself and fear to the city. Similarly the Wolf that afflicts a given urban community is generally the lawless meeting of an out of control need.

St. Francis represents the Christian exercising God's mandated authority in the name of Jesus Christ and working with the cross in view. The Wolf is made both lawful and peaceful through the exercise of spiritual authority and its needs are met through creative problem solving.

St. Francis demonstrates personal mastery and an approach to the Wolf that is entirely different from that of the townsfolk of Gubbio. Francis neither fights nor flees. He has no fear and does not resort to a fight or flight based solution. He faces and confronts the Wolf in order to peacefully master it.

St. Francis demonstrates that even the worst and most lethal of problems have an imaginative solution and that Christian peace making can guide us to a truly beautiful solution. There is a meeting of mutual needs in a climate of mercy. The wolf if he is to change needs food. Indeed we are to feed our enemies! The city if it is to be merciful needs a guarantee of peace. Just covenants are central to peace making and one is forged here. Finally the story tells us that once a problem is tamed it can even be a friend and more than that it can give glory to God.

The St. Francis and The Wolf parable leads us to consider actively engaging in Christian peace making in the urban environment. If we seek to love others in the name of Christ and seek a just peace the answer to the problem will be given to us by God. The very act of seeking to be a peacemaker is creative. Therefore we seek to find peaceful, just, Christian, creative, mastery based and solution-focused answers to the problems that tear cities apart.

An Incarnational Life in the Dominican Cane Fields: Richard

Sometimes the very people you help will try to steal from you, rob you, threaten you life, or even try to kill you. This weekend I was talking to a man who is a real hero in my eyes. Of course he would be the last one to say so. He lives among the poor. He quietly serves the poor. Hundreds of people in his village have received assistance from him in one way or another. The other day a teenager in the village threatened his life...threatened him with a gun. My hero friend was deeply troubled and full of pain and tears. These are moments when one must ask why they are doing this work. If it is for praise, recognition, or anything else that is ego driven, the person will not last. Serving other human beings requires accessing a deeper consciousness that is beyond the ego. It has to be a calling, which means we have heard an inner voice not of this world that speaks to us in times like this when we experience fear. My friend will have to suffer through this time and seek the deeper reasons and listen to the still small voice. We can point to Gandi, Mother Teresa, Martin Luther King Jr. and see that it was not easy to do the right thing and follow one's calling. The people I admire even more are people like my friend who will never get the hero's praise on the scale of famous people. My friend is a man of courage and knows true suffering.

Frank: a teacher from Canada

Frank is 41 years old and has been to the Dominican Republic many times. He comes three times a year, stays in the inclusive resorts. This year he decided to venture out and he said it has changed his life. He has started to see the other side of the Dominican Republic. Yesterday we went to visit poor families in the campo. We spoke to sugar cane workers, visited homes of poor women, spent a few minutes at Mustard Seed, and took pictures with school children. I learned a lot about Frank as I took him around. Frank was an orphan. Born to a mother too young to care for him and then adopted by wonderful people. Frank is grateful for his life and for the many people who love him. When he saw the poverty of people it did not cause him to feel sad or hopeless. He saw it as an opportunity to pay back the many people who have helped him. It is all part of the divine economy of love. Frank also saw the signs of hope in the communities where a small of amount of service and help have made a big difference in the lives of people. He saw that he too could do the same. Frank wants to come back and teach teachers how to teach French and bring a suitcase of bi-lingual books that Canadian schools throw away when they get too old but could be used here. If you want to do big things, think small! Life lesson for the day.

My Incarnational Reasons for Service

My younger brother died on a Sunday. It was not a surprise as he has been ill over the last few years. He had a quadruple heart bypass four years ago. He has not been able to walk for the last couple of years and recently had back surgery. He was 55 years old.

Most of his adult life he lived in Hollywood California. He worked as an extra in more than 50 movies over thirty years. Originally he went to Hollywood as an 18 year old and went to the Don Barnes school of broadcasting. He met a Peruvian immigrant from a very nice family and married. They moved to Washington State where Dennis worked in the radio industry for a couple of years. The marriage did not last and Dennis returned to follow his passion. He left a son behind who is now grown, a former marine, and he is bringing his father's ashes home this week.

My brother and I were abandoned as infants and left in a house in Tacoma, Washington. We were rescued by Lutheran social workers and resided in an orphanage for a period of time. Eventually we were adopted by the people who raised us, our parents. I believe that the people who love you and raise you are your parents. It has little to do with biology and everything to do with love. But it was this latter point that separated by brother and me. He always resented his abandonment. He somehow thought that if he could find his biological parents it would somehow answer his problems. Maybe so! But I was never interested. I figured it was like a pandora's box, afraid of what I might find. I preferred to turn my attention to serving others.

Dennis never gave up on his dream of breaking into the movies. It was not easy and I know he suffered. It was a long and difficult life. One has to admire his persistence and passion. Yes, we could say he was selfish and thinking only of fame and fortune. But who among us is not selfish and yearns for things beyond our reach. None of us is without a certain amount of greed and envy. I know my brother suffered from feelings of abandonment. He craved attention and desired to be validated. It was not his fault he felt this way. It was a product of psychic wounds he suffered early in life. He never got over it. He tried to compensate by seeking the validation of Hollywood. It is fitting that he died the day the annual announcements of the Oscars were in the news.

I know my brother was damaged by our early experiences. He suffered from a mild case of rickets, a lack of vitamin C. It affected his mind and body. As a teenaged he began to exhibit psychotic episodes. It alienated him from kids his own age. I know he was lonely in his youth and pushed him to seek validation even more so. When he got a part in a High School play his senior year, it changed his life. He discovered his passion. We would be so lucky if we would all make such a discovery early in life. It is what we hope for in our children. Still he battled the debilitating wounds of ever increasing mental illness, which I attribute to his early years. I am not an expert in such things but it was quite obvious. Eventually his self medicated with drugs and alcohol and the years went by and Hollywood began to crush him under the weight of rejections. It took a toll on him both physically and mentally and damaged his already fragile state.

I did not see my brother much over the years. Occasionally when I would pass through Los Angeles, I would call him. Often he was drunk and would cuss at me for not warning him. It was painful for both of us. The last time I talked to him was last February. I had been invited to speak at the international Buddhist Christian Conference in Los Angeles. I called to invite him to the hotel where the convention was being held. He was angry again that I called him. It was so sad.

I loved my brother but it had to be from a distance. He blamed me for his life and his failures. I attributed it to the growing illness. When he was sober, he loved to talk to me about UFOs. In later years his story evolved to a memory of having been abducted by aliens. It was his form of spirituality. He felt a kind of validation by these heavenly beings. It was a way of compensating.

Sometimes when I look into the face of the poor, the ill, the troubled, I see my brother. I find a kind of compassion for the Other that I was never able to show to my brother. He would not let me. But maybe I did not try hard enough. Nevertheless I thank him for allowing me to compensate by serving others and in so doing I was serving him.

Mothers: Incarnation of Caring

I believe we are all called to be mothers: men and women. We are called to act with compassion and nurture. This call transcends differences among the sexes.

There are many kinds of mothers in this world. There are good mothers but it is much more difficult when a mother is poor. Shame, desperation, and guilt often invade the souls of women who want to be good mothers but find themselves swallowed up by the circumstances of their situations. Altagracia, is a young mother who sees her child every few days. Most nights she walks the streets of Sosua looking for customers. She is afraid to be seen by people she knows. Her child is passed around to different friends and pseudo-relatives until she returns. Sometimes when she has nothing but a few pesos she returns and buys milk, pampers, and a few balloons for her child to play with. Most of the time she has barely enough money to buy a plastic bag of water. Sometimes the shame is so great she spends her money on alcohol. She knows its wrong but depression and guilt overwhelm her. The men she has had in her life have abandoned her. They certainly do not support her...so she cries..cries for help.

It is easy to be judgmental about such women...easy when you have never had to beg or throw away your self respect. I do not judge these women. When we can help we offer tokens of support, link them to services to meet their present needs for today. There is no tomorrow.

We just celebrated Mother's Day in North America. It is too easy to be sentimental, too easy when there are women who cannot have children but want them, women who find motherhood a trial, to easy to think only of the ideal when some of these women do not have the resources to live. They are walking wounded, bearing sufferings that are symbolized in all our great religions both secular and sacred. No matter how we see these situations there are the innocent children. They did not ask to be born into this world in such circumstances. This is where we must focus our compassion in the end.

Dorothy Day, the co founder of the Worker's Movement, saw in these women the face of her Savior, the same suffering, doubts, struggle to do the right thing. She served many of these women and children in the ghettos of the United States. For me she is a model of how I am to live and how I need to call others to live in the same way. She lived in solidarity with the poor. She took pride in the fact that she was often mistaken for a homeless women. Volunteers in her soup kitchens often did not recognize her. This is the face of service to others.

Here in the Dominican Republic there is a women's organization called MUDA. Women helping other women. This is a real solution to many of these problems and an effective way to ultimately help women like Altagracia. The other day I visited a women's workshop in Puerto Plata. There they were training women to upholster furniture. I was thrilling to see the hope and joy in these women's faces who were developing real skills. The staff was excellent and using effective teaching techniques. Of course I saw some of the problems ahead. How would they find employment? Would they have access to credit to start their own business? Would they be exploited by business people who would probably not pay them a living wage? In spite of all these potential pitfalls, it is a great beginning, and a way for these women to get off the street.

Afterward

After several years of work, I have finished a translation of the life of Joshua the Stylite. Originally written in Syriac in the 6th century, it is one of our earliest histories written by an eye witness on the Persian Roman Wars. Joshua in his early years sat atop a stone column. This was a religious curiosity in the 5th and 6th century in Syria. Simeon was noted to have sat on top of his pole or column for 44 years.

These men were odd. They attracted attention by their extreme behavior. Sometimes I feel like these men. After all I have worked for years in remote regions of the world doing things that few people would ever do. Yet, from their vantage point, high atop their columns, these men were able to marshal political and religious forces of their day to act with compassion for the poor and needy of the region. In the same way I feel that many of us who work for human rights, the alleviation of hunger and poverty, in the DR are able to do the same. It is prophetic work. Like Elijah, Elisha, and Jeremiah they pointed out the injustices of their day. They did not solve every crime, or remedy every injustice, or heal every disease. They pointed out a few examples as a divine witness to what we are all called to do at some level. We are doing the same here in the DR. No, we are not feeding every hungry child, healing every sick person, or providing an education for every child without opportunity. We are only helping a few, but that is enough to be a witness, a prophetic example to the larger culture. In fact, to try to feed every hungry family would be counter productive. We would enable the Dominican institutions to sit back and let others do their work. It is the responsibility of the government and the people themselves to care for one another. You cannot get people to be responsible when you do all the work for them. But pointing the way by building modules of examples with programs that are efficient, compassionate, and productive is the way to inspire the larger population to do the right thing. This is what the "Stylite" or "pole sitters" did in the 6th century. Their example shows us the way.

Meditation for Workers Among the Poor

This is who we are and what we do:

We plant seeds but we do not make them grow.

We water plants already alive, knowing that they will bloom into future promise.

We build things that will need further development.

We strike a spark in the minds of children that will produce effects beyond our imagination.

We cannot do everything and there is a sense of freedom in knowing this truth.

It enables us to do something instead of nothing.

It may be incomplete, but it is a beginning, a tiny effort in a big project, an opportunity for God's grace to complete the dream.

We may never see the finished result of our labor, but that is the difference between the Lord and the laborer.

We are laborers, not Lords, ministers, not Messiahs.

We are prophets of a dream that belongs to others.

How to Serve the Poor

1. Christian spirituality is visualized in the Eucharist, a life shared with others in imitation of broken bread.

2. Offering bread in love or pity to the poor can either raise up or oppress a person.

3. At its root, there is only one reason for the existence of poverty: the absence of selfless love. Become selfless against poverty."

4. In our work with the poor, we must be transformed from pity to compassion, from pathos to justice.

5. Every suffering person we encounter in life is waiting to be embraced by God's compassion. Therefore, we must become the arms and hands of God in the world. This is what it means to become Christ."

6. Holiness is social work because it reveals itself in love and justice."

7. "Every act of mercy given and received draws us closer to the presence of God."

8. Prayer without works of mercy was inconceivable to Jesus."

9. All acts of service to the poor are acts of obedience to demonstrate the presence of God's love."

essentially acts of obedience - that is, we are doing w love and mercy."

10. When we relieve the pain and suffering of others, we realize God's love."

"The best way to love God is to relieve the pain and suffering of others."

Projects of Dominican Outreach

Census on Homeless Children

1) Census Project for homeless children: perhaps this has been our most successful program as we have been operating feeding centers in various barrios of Puerto Plata. Children and women come to the centers where we not only feed them but take information on their medical needs, living conditions, reports of abuse, and educational needs. We put this data into a database that we share with other faith-based organizations as well as the government social service offices that are almost non-existent and under-funded. We use this data to identify the most needy homeless children and refer them to an orphanage for homeless boys that just started this year. Next year we hope to participate in starting an orphanage for girls. Our costs run about $105.00 a week.

2) Through our census project we have identified dozens of women who have children and are in the later stages of HIV/AIDS infection. Because many of them are Haitian Economic immigrants from across the border, they have no access to medical care or help of any kind. We call this our 2) Milk and Pampers Project: we distribute canned milk to dozens of mothers who have been diagnosed with HIV/AIDS who have children 1-5 years old. It puts us into weekly contact with these women so when they become too sick we can intervene and find places for their children. We work with a local judge to find homes for the children. The Pampers are highly desired by these mothers. When you are poor, it is difficult to get access to clean water, energy to wash properly, and dispose of human waste. Pampers are making some of these hygene problems easier for these women. When we have excess Pampers we donate them to the Mustard Seed orphanage for disabled children where there are about 18 children who are mostly bedridden and brain damaged. Many have been recovered from toilets and garbage bins where they have been left to die. A missionary group from Jamaica supplies the workers who care for these children.

Puerto Plata Kids

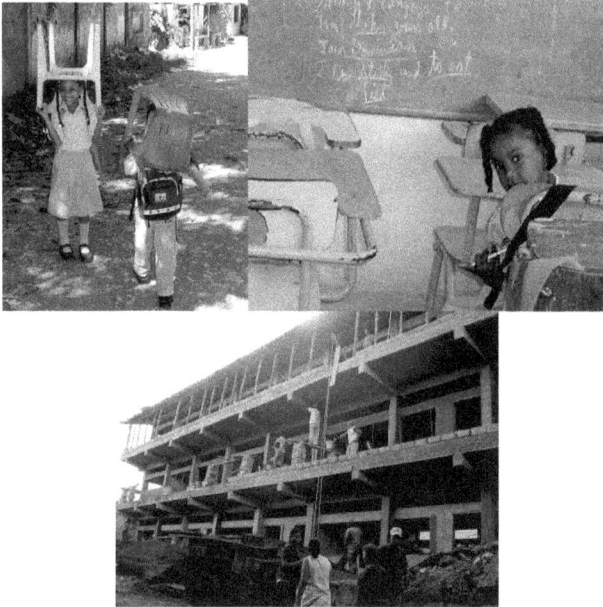

3) Our third project is " Education Intervention" which has two thrusts: first we have a teacher training project which has received seed money from a Canadian couple in Brandon, Manitoba who are sponsoring the building of a teacher laboratory. This is a fully equipped classroom where we will start this Fall (2007) to train teachers from schools in the barrios on better methods of teaching. We will use Master Dominican Teachers and volunteer teachers from North America to do the training. Most teachers here do not have university educations and most are appointed by local political parties. Many teachers are simply the older sisters and brothers in a community. Nevertheless, we have found many inspiring people who have the gift of teaching and we will help them with continuing education workshops for teachers starting in October when our teacher laboratory is finished. The second thrust of our education endeavor is direct support of poor children who need uniforms, backpacks, and supplies to go to school. Thousands of children are blocked from going to school here because they do not have the $20 a month to go

to public school. Poverty often pushes them onto the street at an average age of 10 years old to shine shoes, sell food, or beg to help support family members.

Micro-Credit Project

4) We have just begun a micro credit project with our first family. Many families on the North Coast of the Dominican Republic have subsistence occupations. Fishing families live from day to day. Recently we received a small gift from a member of the Canadian Royal Mounted Police who wanted to help one family. So we met with a cooperative of fishing families. With the help of two other organizations we loaned money to the cooperative to buy a boat motor. This will allow one family to move out of poverty on the condition that they pay back the loan with the increased income they generate from the benefit of the boat motor. World-wide these micro-credit programs are highly successful. Banks will not loan to the poor but groups like the Mennonites and others here in the Dominican Republic have helped several hundred families rise out of poverty and subsistence living through private managed loans. Our census work ties in nicely with this work as we discover many worthy people who simply need someone to believe in them.

To participate in these programs as a volunteer or donor please see www. Geocities.com/dominicanoutreach

www.ingramcontent.com/pod-product-compliance
Lightning Source LLC
Chambersburg PA
CBHW021333090426
42742CB00008B/589